Elizabeth Williams Champney

Three Vassar Girls in Switzerland

Elizabeth Williams Champney

Three Vassar Girls in Switzerland

ISBN/EAN: 9783337173500

Printed in Europe, USA, Canada, Australia, Japan

Cover: Foto ©ninafisch / pixelio.de

More available books at **www.hansebooks.com**

THREE VASSAR GIRLS IN SWITZERLAND.

THREE VASSAR GIRLS.

BY

ELIZABETH W. CHAMPNEY.

THREE VASSAR GIRLS ABROAD.
THREE VASSAR GIRLS IN ENGLAND.
THREE VASSAR GIRLS IN SOUTH AMERICA.
THREE VASSAR GIRLS IN ITALY.
THREE VASSAR GIRLS ON THE RHINE.
THREE VASSAR GIRLS AT HOME.
THREE VASSAR GIRLS IN FRANCE.
THREE VASSAR GIRLS IN RUSSIA AND TURKEY.
THREE VASSAR GIRLS IN SWITZERLAND.

ESTES & LAURIAT, Publishers,
BOSTON, MASS.

AT THE ALTDORF FESTIVAL.

THREE VASSAR GIRLS

IN

SWITZERLAND.

BY

ELIZABETH W. CHAMPNEY,

AUTHOR OF "A NEGLECTED CORNER OF EUROPE," "THREE VASSAR GIRLS ABROAD,"
"THREE VASSAR GIRLS IN ENGLAND," ETC.

ILLUSTRATED BY "CHAMP"
AND OTHER DISTINGUISHED ARTISTS.

BOSTON:
ESTES & LAURIAT,
PUBLISHERS.

CONTENTS.

CHAPTER		PAGE
I.	A Skeleton Key and Margaret's Mistake	11
II.	Annette's Revenge	20
III.	Geneva	34
IV.	The Countess	51
V.	The Jungfrau and the Oberland	72
VI.	Lucerne	90
VII.	The Tell Festival	106
VIII.	Our Lady of Poverty	123
IX.	Life at the Alm	143
X.	Lost	158
XI.	The Wagner Festival. Bavaria	177
XII.	The Fairy Cow	192
XIII.	The Great St. Bernard and Mont Blanc	205
XIV.	The Fête des Vignerons	222

ILLUSTRATIONS.

	PAGE
At the Altdorf Festival	3
Margaret	12
Annette	13
The Castle of Weierburg	15
St. Cecilia as Mediator	21
Grandfather Houghton	24
A Swiss Mountain Torrent	25
An Alpine Waterfall	27
"Do You want to go to Prison or to Switzerland?"	31
Grandfather Houghton in Alpine Costume	37
"Mer de Glace," Mont Blanc	39
Alice Newton	41
The Girl in the Hading Veil	42
Calumet and Hecla	43
Lord Highnose	44
Mr. Walker	45
The Hotel Neuchatelois	46
The Prisoner of Chillon	47
The Countess	52
Lajos	54
"Calumet and Hecla is up!"	57
Peasant Waitress	58
The Dent du Midi from above the Lake of Geneva	59
The Countess enthroned	65
The Entomologist receives the Apology	68
A Metamorphosed Native of Interlaken	76
The Jungfrau	77
The Judge salutes the Jungfrau	78

	PAGE
"Positively Fwiteful!"	82
The Wellhorn and Wetterhorn	85
Mr. Barney Jones in Difficulties	88
Pilatus, Lake of Lucerne	91
Hotel National, Lucerne	93
Stock Quotations	96
Annette takes her Departure	99
Bridge of Lucerne	102
Margaret and Alice discuss Lajos	109
The Rigi, from Lucerne	111
A Swiss Maiden	113
Tell's Chapel, Lake of Lucerne	114
Costume of Peasant of Unterwalden	116
Railway up the Rigi	119
The Comforts of Donkey-riding	121
On the Brink of a Precipice	124
The Matterhorn	125
Katchen	132
Yakob Lochwalder	133
A Goatherd of the Zermatt Valley	139
Yakob accepts his Relatives	145
The Accident on the Matterhorn	149
The Real Thing at last	156
The Great Aletsch Glacier	163
Mother Lochwalder	166
Rescuing Party on the Matterhorn	169
On the Matterhorn	170
Abbey of Einsiedeln	179
Frau Selig	182
Minna	183

	PAGE
A Devotee of Wagner	184
Listening to "Parsifal," No. 1	185
Listening to "Parsifal," No. 2	185
Mrs. Newton	187
On the Fichtelgebirge	188
Nikolas	197
A Peasant of Zermatt	199
A Peasant Woman of the Zermatt Valley	201
The Great St. Bernard	209
Barry, the Brave Dog of St. Bernard	213
The Baron	217
Baroness of Hohenschlosse	217
"To think that I was like that!"	218
A Student of Berne	224
High Street, Berne	225
Katchen Americanized	227
At the Festival	228
Taking it all in	229
Vintage Festival, Vevey	231
Kisfaludy Janos	233

THREE VASSAR GIRLS

IN

SWITZERLAND.

CHAPTER I.

A SKELETON KEY AND MARGARET'S MISTAKE.

"AND to think that by a word it is in my power to prove her the grand-niece of a baroness."

The speaker was Annette Stauffer, a Swiss girl, ex-seamstress and waitress in Margaret's home. She spoke to herself, excitedly, as she rapidly packed her trunk, for she had just given up her situation.

"Shall I furnish the missing link in the chain of evidence, and prove her the child of one of the proudest houses of Austria? No; she is arrogant enough as she is. She has treated me as if I were the earth to be trodden upon. She is a bundle of selfishness, through and through. She cares for no one but herself. If it were Miss Boylston, so kind and thoughtful of others, so gentle and so generous, I would work my fingers to stubs to serve her; but My Lady Disdain, *never*."

Annette was wrong. Margaret was not wholly selfish. She possessed magnificent qualities, capabilities of self-sacrifice and devotion; but these were as yet undeveloped, and hidden under the crust of a love of ease. It was true that she was haughty, and apt to exhibit a fine scorn of everything mean and base; but the scorn was more frequently excited by moral meanness than by low rank in the social scale. Rank of intellect and heroism commanded an almost overweening admiration from her, and it was her special heartburn that none of her own family had distinguished themselves in any way. She would have liked to be a leader in society for some real merit of her own, or of her ancestors; and she was a leader among her friends and associates both at home and at college, for the good and sufficient reason of ability. The name of Margaret Duffey figured as President of the Philalethean Society, President of the Young Women's Christian Association, President of the Tennis Club, of the Dramatic Association, of her class, Senior Editor of the *Miscellany*, and Chairman of the Executive Committee of half a dozen other organizations. It was a vexation to her that it was such a plebeian name — Margaret Duffey! It had a genuine Irish sound. One would imagine, on reading it, that it belonged to a laundress. She had said this before Annette, and the sewing-woman's gray eyes had snapped viciously. "She despises all the laboring class," Annette thought, "and me with the rest." But Margaret was not thinking of Annette at all. "What makes it all the more vexatious," she added, speaking to her friend Cecilia Boylston, familiarly called Saint, who was visiting her that summer, "is the fact that it is not really our name at all. Grandfather came to this country a political refugee, and changed his name to preserve his *incognito*. He might have chosen a pleasanter appellation, when he had so unlimited a choice. When father was a boy he was told our real name; but would you believe it, he

MARGARET.

attached so little importance to it that he forgot it. He can only remember that it sounded like Duffey, but was more aristocratic."

"Did your grandfather leave no relatives in Europe?" Cecilia asked, while Annette, who was sewing in the corner, pricked up her ears.

"Yes; there was a little sister Margaret, of whom he was very fond. When I was born he insisted that father should name me for her, and he wrote to her of my birth. Grandfather was an old man then, and when the reply to the letter came from my great-aunt he lay on his death-bed. He charged my father to keep it for me, as it might prove to my advantage some day."

"Surely, Margaret, this letter must give you all the information you wish."

ANNETTE.

"Information! That is just what it does not give. It is full of expressions of affection for her dear elder brother, for the nephew whom she had never seen, and for the little namesake, who, she hopes, will some day visit her god-mother. But the letter is dated, simply, 'The Riffel,' and signed 'Greta.' I know that The Riffel is in Switzerland; but father has an impression that we are not of Swiss extraction. I have a picture of the Weierburg, which I fancy looks like the home which she describes."

Annette listened greedily. She longed to see the letter of which

Margaret spoke, for her own home was near Zermatt and the Riffelburg. "Perhaps I knew her great-aunt, or at least, could help to find her," she said to herself; but she did not mention this to Margaret, or ask to see the letter. This was not her way of procedure.

She fancied that when she was not present people must be talking about her, and she listened at keyholes to learn what they were saying. Pierre, the gardener, meant, simply, that she had a suspicious nature, when he remarked that Annette was "naturally surreptitious"; but the statement was perfectly true as it stood. It was not possible for Annette to be frank and open-handed. She was frightfully cross-eyed, and watched you narrowly, when she appeared to be interested in something in the opposite direction, and this physical defect seemed to have affected her character. She had a cross-eyed way of accomplishing all her designs. She was consumed with curiosity to ascertain Margaret's ancestry, and she would ascertain it; but Margaret should never know that it interested her in the least. So she sewed the ruche into Margaret's best gown, and thought with glee of the skeleton key in her pocket, and that she would have two good hours to rummage for that letter, while the young ladies were at the lawn party, for Mrs. Duffey was away from home. She needed all the time; for it was not in the little secretary through which she looked first, nor in the safe under the stairs with the silver, nor in the japanned tin box in which Mr. Duffey kept his stocks and bonds, or in any of the bureau drawers, or behind the sliding panel over the mantel, a secret hiding-place where Mrs. Duffey kept her jewels, which Annette had discovered the second day after her arrival; but it dropped at last out of the atlas where Margaret had carelessly left it in searching for The Riffel. Annette sat down and read eagerly. The letter was written in a delicate foreign script, in Austrian-German, very easy for Annette, but puzzling for Margaret to decipher. It ran as follows: —

THE CASTLE OF WEIERBURG.

"RIFFELHAUS, SWITZERLAND, July, ——

"MY DEAR BROTHER,— I cannot tell you how overjoyed I am to receive your letter. I had not heard from you for so long, that my heart imagined many tragedies. And so I am a great-aunt? That sounds almost like a grandmother. The honor comes to me early, owing to the great difference in our ages. Only a child when you went away to America, but I remember the sorrowful day very clearly still. There are some things which are so branded into our memories that we can never forget them.

"But the little girl! I am glad that she has come, and that you have named her for me. My god-daughter as well as grand-niece. Some day, now that our calamities seem to be overpast, she must come to her Aunt Greta. I shall not be such a very old woman when she is grown. I hope she will want to come to me. Tell her the way to the old home beside the mountain, with the window overhanging the precipice, from which they say you used to fish for swallows, with a fish-line, when a boy. Tell her all your old haunts, and I will show them to her. How you used to love to hang over that balcony! I remember that once you rescued a little dog that had fallen into the valley. You made a slip-noose, the loop of which was a handkerchief, and, passing it over his body, drew him up to your window. A few days since, I saw a peasant girl of Zermatt draw a lamb out of the torrent which ran under her balcony, in much the same way, and the action reminded me so of you that I brought her home with me as my maid"—

There had been something familiar to Annette in the story as Margaret had told it; but with the incident of the lamb it all came back to her. Without any doubt, the Austrian Baroness who spent that same summer, eighteen years ago, at the Riffelhaus, with whom Annette, then a young peasant girl, served as maid, was Margaret's great-aunt. She remembered rescuing the lamb, and that she did it, not from any feeling of mercy, but because she was fond of roast mutton. To make assurance doubly sure, there was the Baroness's crest on the waxen seal, so indistinct that Margaret had not made it out, but Annette could trace the firebrand held by a gauntleted hand.

And how like Margaret was to her god-mother, — the same imperious manners. Strange that she had not noticed the likeness before, — and as fond of riding on horse back. So absorbed was Annette in the letter that she did not hear a light step on the stair, or look up until Margaret stood before her and snatched the letter from her hands in a rage of indignation. "What do you mean by reading my letters?" she exclaimed. "How dare you? And my desk open! How did you manage that? What? A skeleton key! Annette, you are a thief."

Annette sprang to her feet, the color flaming into her pale face.

"I am not. What have I stolen? Look in my trunk, look in my room, look everywhere."

"I do not care to look. I am not one of the prying kind."

"I demand it. You called me a thief. Prove that it is so, or else you lie. What have you ever missed?"

The two angry women stood facing each other as Cecilia entered the room with a calm, "What is the matter?"

Margaret showed the skeleton key, and told her story.

"Appearances are against you, Annette," said Cecilia. "What explanation have you to offer? What possible need has an honest woman of a skeleton key?"

"My brother was a locksmith; he made it for me, so I need not trouble myself with a great many keys, — one for my trunk, another for my room, another for my bureau."

"Very convenient; and equally so for all of our locks, I presume." This from Margaret, in her most sneering accents.

"Be it so. I ask again, what have you ever missed? I have been with you four years. I could with that key unlock your safe, your father's money-box, your mother's jewel-case, everything, — that is true, — but what has been stolen since I lived with you — nothing — "

"Is this true?" Cecilia asked.

"I believe it is," Margaret replied. "I have been too hasty, and I apologize. You are no thief, Annette; but you are what I despise just as much, — a prying, spying, suspicious eavesdropper. No; you needn't speak up. I stumbled over you the other day, in the entry, when I opened the door more quickly than you expected. You were listening, and you can't deny it. I absolve you from any intention of stealing. It was probably curiosity, and nothing else, which led you to ransack my desk and read my letters. If not, what motive had you for spying into my affairs? Are you a special detective?"

There was only one way for Annette to vindicate herself, and she told a part of the truth.

"I heard what you said this morning, Miss Margaret, of a letter from your great-aunt, from The Riffel. You know I come from that region; and I wanted to see if possibly I knew her, and I found that I did."

"What, you knew my Aunt Greta?" Margaret exclaimed excitedly. "Tell me about her! Is she alive? Can I find her?"

It was Annette's turn to triumph. "I knew her, I could help you find her; but you have called me a thief, you have resented my prying into your affairs. I will have nothing more to do with them. I leave your mother's employ to-day. You may tell her why. But I shall call, on Saturday, for my wages, and for a recommendation for *honesty*, Miss Margaret, for honesty, and for minding my own business. Do you understand?"

CHAPTER II.

ANNETTE'S REVENGE.

WHEN Margaret became sufficiently calm to consider the matter coolly, she felt that she had made a great mistake in allowing her temper to make an enemy of Annette.

"My angry passions are always getting me into trouble," she said remorsefully. "I can never learn to hold my tongue, and count an hundred. And now I shall never find my fairy god-mother."

"Perhaps it was only a piece of bravado on Annette's part, by way of revenge."

"No; she is truthful as well as honest, and not quick at invention. There was too much genuine triumph in her eyes. I have narrowly missed a great piece of good fortune."

"If you really regret having spoken as you did, why don't you go right to her and apologize?"

"It would be of no use. But Saint, dear, she dotes on you; intercede for me."

With many misgivings, Cecilia tapped at Annette's door. "Who's there?" was the ungracious response; but on hearing Cecilia's voice, the maid unbarred the door. Her eyes were red, and her cheeks swollen; she had been weeping passionately. Cecilia put her arms about her and gently soothed her. "Margaret is very sorry," she said, after a time. "Will you not forgive her?"

The girl stiffened instantly. "If Miss Margaret is sorry, why does she not come and say so?"

"She will, if you will let her—"

"She can do as she pleases; it makes no difference to me."

"But it makes a difference to Margaret. She has a good heart, and regrets that she has caused you pain."

Annette sniffed scornfully. Cecilia remained with her some time longer, but could only make her agree not to leave the house until Mrs. Duffey's return that evening.

There was a family council on the arrival of Mr. and Mrs. Duffey. Seated around the library table, they discussed the matter in all its bearings, while Annette listened in the entry.

Mr. Duffey was of the opinion that the girl's freaks were not worthy of consideration. "I have lived without my precious relative all my life, and I can do without her now. If she had cared for me in all these years, she might have looked me up."

"But her kind letter was never answered, was it, Theodore?" asked gentle Mrs. Duffey. "She must have thought that it never reached its destination, or that we did not care to keep up friendly relations."

ST. CECILIA AS MEDIATOR.

"It was never answered, because, when it arrived, father was too feeble in mind to attend to it, and he was the only one who knew the address. She was only staying for a short time at the Riffel Hotel; and I have no idea where the old home that she speaks of is. It may be in the neighborhood, and it may be miles away. It is my opinion that Annette knows nothing about the matter."

"It seems strange to me, father," said Margaret, "that you never inquired more about your family from grandpa."

"Father very early showed me that such inquiries were useless. 'I am a proscribed man, by no fault of my own, under penalty of death,' he confided to me. 'I have no longer any country or antecedents, no home or family, except that which I can found here. The past is closed behind us; let us look only to the future.' If I had known more, I might have endangered his life; but having no secrets in my possession, I could not divulge them. I have reason to believe that letters not unfrequently passed between my father and his sister; but hers were always carefully destroyed. This is the only one which has been preserved."

"And this looks forward to a happy meeting with the little Greta, 'now that our calamities are overpast.'"

"I used to think she might come to this country," said Mr. Duffey; "and I confess there was no great pleasure in the anticipation. After I had the honor of so respectable a connection as with your mother's family, I used to wonder what my honored father-in-law would say if a Nihilistic female with a carpet-bag full of dynamite should some day dismount from an omnibus at our doors, and exclaim, 'I am your long-lost aunt!' I tell you what, Greta, you had better let well enough alone. Your great-aunt is an unknown quantity, and we are very happy as we are."

"But your father was not a criminal," Mrs. Duffey remarked. "He was a perfect gentleman, Theodore; and my father respected him highly. Whatever his misfortune, it was no fault of his, I am sure."

"And if aunt is an unknown quantity, there is the possibility that she may be a lady of rank," Margaret suggested, "a baroness, perhaps—" (There was a slight noise in the entry.) "And at any rate, we shall ascertain what our real name is; and it can't be worse than Duffey."

"There is only one chance out of a million of your drawing a prize," Mr. Duffey insisted, practically. "Suppose you discover some very undesirable relatives, if not actual criminals, — poor, ignorant peasants. This Aunt Greta is an old woman by this time. Imagine her poverty-stricken, disagreeable, diseased —"

Then for an instant Margaret showed her better nature. "In that case, father, is there no duty laid on us? We have enough and to spare. Is it not dishonest for us to leave a relative in possible need?"

Mr. Duffey looked at his daughter in surprised admiration. "And if she needs more than money? I could furnish that, — but if she needs personal care and attention?"

"I think you would find that I would not fail." Margaret spoke modestly but firmly; but Annette in the entry gave so loud a sniff of scornful doubt, that Mrs. Duffey started.

"Did you hear that noise? It reminded me of a snake in the grass."

"More likely a rat in the arras, à la Hamlet," replied Margaret, pointing significantly at the entry door. No one sprang to open it; all were agreed that the best policy now was conciliation.

"And do you agree with your daughter's sentiments?" asked Mr. Duffey.

"Certainly," replied his wife. "Only prove that she is your aunt, and I will receive any one."

"I wonder whether the Judge would agree with you."

"I think it would be better to consult with father, of course," said Mrs. Duffey; "he has such excellent judgment."

It was at once decided to adjourn the council to the home of Mrs. Duffey's father.

The family found Judge Houghton deeply immersed in making jottings from his scrap-book collection of the "Doings of the New York Geographical Society." So absorbed was he that, ordinarily punctilious, he had forgotten to take off his high hat. He greeted them all effusively, however, and began to talk at once.

"I am arranging for my summer vacation," he said briskly; "and I have been looking over all the lectures that have been given before our society. I want to do something this summer that I can utilize in a lecture, with stereopticon views, at Chickering Hall this winter; and I have decided that the Higher Alps are just what I want. Don't some of you want to go with me? Mother, here, thinks she is too old for mountaineering."

GRANDFATHER HOUGHTON.

"I will go with you, grandpa," Margaret spoke up promptly. "At least, as far as The Riffel, if that's in your itinerary."

"The very place to start from for the best mountaineering: just at the foot of the Matterhorn and the Weisshorn and Monte Rosa, and Mont Blanc within a stone's throw, so to speak.

"Only look at this panorama outlined in Baedeker, of the view from the Gorner Grat, near the Riffel Hotel, and listen while I read a description of it from William H. Rideing.

"'On the one side the broad stream of the Gorner Glacier sweeps along beneath our feet, and across it rise the huge mountains by which the ice stream is augmented: Monte Rosa — Queen of the Alps — with her coronet of peaks; the wedge-like mass of the Lyskamm; the Snowy Twins (Castor and Pollux); and the long, craggy ridge of the white-capped Breithorn. Then comes a break, as the eye sweeps over

A SWISS MOUNTAIN TORRENT.

the plateau traversed by the well-known Théodule Pass, to rest on the grandest sight in all the Alps, the marvellous Matterhorn, seen in one

AN ALPINE WATERFALL.

of its most impressive aspects, — an obelisk of snow-flecked rock, four thousand feet in height. Beyond this comes another company of giants, the peaks from the Dent Blanche to the Weisshorn. There is no spot in the whole of the Alps, accessible with such ease, which commands a grander panoramic view; nothing of the kind surpasses in grandeur and beauty its circle of peaks and glaciers.'

"There, Margaret, have you followed me carefully, and found all the names mentioned on the outline?"

"Yes, grandpa."

"Well, The Riffel is just the locality for me to take as my centre of operations. I am glad you have been thinking of the same place."

"I really think some one ought to go with you and take care of you, father," said Mrs. Duffey. "Margaret is just the one. You can make a great many excursions together. She's a great walker."

"I know it, I know it," exclaimed the old gentleman in high glee.

"Margaret will have her hands full," said anxious Mrs. Houghton. "You are entirely too old, John, to go trampoozling over the mountains, when you might rest your bones comfortably at home."

"Too old! Look at the other members of the club! I'm an infant compared with the best travellers."

"That is true," replied Margaret; "it is a most venerable assemblage. When I look down upon it from the gallery, the bald heads have the appearance of white stones peeping up above water from a ford. I often imagine myself skipping from one to the other, across the entire length of the hall."

"You dreadful child! Is there no Prophet Elisha, to call down a troop of bears, to punish such irreverence?"

"No, grandpa; and the bears are too busy, down in Wall Street, to care for naughty me. But listen while we tell you why I have decided to go to Switzerland this summer."

"I did not know you had decided," said Mr. Duffey. "I thought it was to be submitted to your Grandfather Houghton; and I am sure he will disapprove."

But Judge Houghton, influenced, possibly, to some extent, by his own desire to avail himself of so lively a travelling companion, looked on the scheme with favor.

"We need not commit ourselves to anything," he said. "We can simply find out, or try to find out, the truth. The first thing to do is to ascertain what Annette really knows. Have you made it up with her, Margaret?"

"I am afraid not, grandpa. This miserable business has taught me to try to keep a tighter rein on my temper. I went to her, after Saint had labored with her, and apologized; but she would not utter one syllable. I am afraid she will not help us."

"We will see," said the Judge. "I'll dine with you to-morrow. Let me deal with her."

"But will she remain?" asked Margaret. "She only promised Saint to stay until she had spoken with you, mamma."

"I have given her no opportunity to speak with me, as yet," said Mrs. Duffey. "I think we can manage an interview."

Annette, after her white heat of passion had subsided, was not anxious to lose her good situation; but her decision that she would not to carry into effect her threat of leaving the family, did not argue any forgiveness of Margaret. On the contrary, she was convinced that she could better revenge herself by remaining near her, and that neither the pincers of the Inquisition, nor any amount of kindness, would either wrest or coax from her the information which was so much desired.

It will therefore be readily understood that Judge Houghton, with all his legal wile and acumen, had a difficult subject to handle.

He began in a conciliatory way, and assumed that Annette would gladly assist them, for a little compensation.

"You are a good girl, Annette," he remarked; "and I understand that you send back a very large proportion of your earnings to your family in Switzerland. You are doubtless very fond of them. When do you propose to go back for a visit."

Annette answered, very truly, that, much as she desired this, she was too poor to think of even a steerage passage.

"Ah!" exclaimed the delighted strategist. "Then you will be pleased to learn that I contemplate taking a trip to Switzerland, with my granddaughter, this summer, and I would be very glad to engage your services as her maid. All expenses paid, my good Annette, both going and returning, and a vacation for you, after we are fairly installed in some pleasant hotel, — a vacation of several weeks, in which you can visit your family. How would you like that?"

Annette's eyes shot forth a momentary gleam of pleasure, but a cold gray sheath of suspicion was instantly drawn over them.

"And in return?" she asked.

"Oh! In return, you could render my granddaughter any trifling services she might require, as lady's maid and companion. You know the language, and the country, the best routes, the regular fares, and all that sort of thing. You could be of great service to us in enabling us to dispense with a courier. And then, another thing, — my granddaughter's main object in visiting Switzerland is to look up her father's family. Perhaps you could help us in discovering them."

"Perhaps? But certainly I could help you, — if I wished. Is that one of the trifling services of which you spoke, to be included in my duties as lady's maid?"

"No, no. That, of course, should have special compensation. If you enable us to discover Margaret's great-aunt, I will pay the passage of any two of your own relatives who may want to emigrate to America. Come, now; isn't that generous?"

"It is sufficiently generous."

"Then it's a bargain?"

"No, sir."

"What conditions do you ask?"

"I will not do it on any conditions."

"Indeed! Highty-tighty, young woman, better think that over

again. Do you know I can make you give me this information? Perhaps you would prefer being committed to prison, to this tour of which we have just been speaking?"

"No one can compel me to speak; and I can keep my own counsel."

"But this isn't your own counsel. That's the point. You have, or pretend to have, valuable knowledge."

"I have it."

"Very well. You have information valuable to my client, which you refuse to render. It is hers by right of law; and the law takes you in hand in the same way as if you were withholding other valuables from her. Now, what are you going to do about it? Don't be a fool, Annette. Consider your own interests. Do you want to go to prison, or do you want to go to Switzerland? Answer me that."

Annette was a coward. She did not doubt Judge Houghton's power to imprison her for life; and she was just about to surrender, when Margaret entered the library, and Judge Houghton repeated the alternatives, as he had set them before the girl.

"DO YOU WANT TO GO TO PRISON OR TO SWITZERLAND?"

"No, Annette," Margaret exclaimed impulsively. "I will not allow you to be prosecuted, even if you insist on keeping this secret from me; but I beg of you to be magnanimous, and to help me find my aunt. Think how you would feel under the same circumstances."

Annette looked up. Apparently, she was regarding the stuffed owl on the top of the bookcase; in reality, she was studying Margaret with intense malice.

"How do you know that you will thank me, when you have found her? She may not be the grand lady you expect."

"Then, so much the more is it a sacred duty on my part. Annette, I shall never blame you, whatever be the result."

"Suppose she is dead, or moved away, so that I cannot find her?"

"I shall not blame you for that, either."

"Then I call you and Judge Houghton to witness that you bring it all on yourself; that I did not want to undertake this business, but that, between you, you make me do it."

Annette did not yield from any magnanimity. She had no faith in Margaret's assurance that she would not be imprisoned if she persisted in her refusal. Moreover, she had really decided not to aid in the discovery; but apparent yielding would extricate her from her present disagreeable position, and give her time to think of some mode of evading the issue.

So, while Margaret thanked and praised her effusively, she maintained a stony silence, still simulating an intense interest in the stuffed owl.

"And now," said Judge Houghton, "that these preliminaries have been satisfactorily settled, let us proceed to the real matter in hand. Will you be so good as to tell us, Annette, all that you know of my granddaughter's great-aunt? In the first place, how did you happen to know my granddaughter's relative?"

Annette related the circumstances of her engagement as maid.

"And what was the lady's name?"

Margaret bent forward eagerly. The hated name of Duffey was about to be lifted. Annette saw the intense expectation, and she could not satisfy it at that moment, if her life had depended upon it.

"No," she exclaimed, a hysterical sob rising in her throat; "not now, not now. I have told enough, I have endured enough. I have promised to help you find her; but it must be in my own way. Let me go. I can stand no more." And turning abruptly, she left the room.

Judge Houghton looked after her in astonishment, "Well, this is a most extraordinary young person!" he exclaimed.

"Annette is peculiar," Margaret answered. "You have gained a great concession; and it will not do to press her too far. Let her take her own way, and we shall lose nothing by it."

But in her own room Annette was going through another of her rages. "I never shall tell her, never! If it were Miss Boylston, yes; but Miss Margaret! I will go to prison first. She thinks, now, that her aunt may be poor and mean. Let her torment herself with that idea. If she only were a beggar, or a *cretin!* She says that she would accept her, whatever her condition. I would like to see her put to the test. What would my lady do if she should find that her relatives were of the peasant class? Her aunt an old crone like my grandmother, living in a den like our *châlet?* She thinks that she would accept the situation, would not be ashamed of her relations, and would bring the old aunt back with her to America. She would do nothing of the kind. I would ask no sweeter revenge than to see her look of horror on making a discovery like that."

Annette paused in her monologue. An electrifying idea had suddenly struck her, and she stood transfixed, then clapped her hands three times over her head, and laughed like a mad woman. She had found her revenge.

CHAPTER III.

GENEVA.

"Within the Switzer's varied land.
When summer chases high the snow,
You'll meet with many a youthful band
Of strangers wandering to and fro;
Through hamlet, town, and healing bath,
They haste, and rest as chance may call.
No day without its mountain path.
No path without its waterfall."
             LORD HOUGHTON.

ALL were surprised, the next day, to see Annette of her own accord ask for another interview, and to hear her volunteer the most helpful information. She said that Margaret's great-aunt was known in Zermatt by the name of Madame Lochwalder; but she, Annette, pretended to suspect that this was an assumed name. Her real one she professed not to know. She felt sure that she was still living at Zermatt, for her uncle had mentioned in his last letter that Madame Lochwalder had bought his mountain *châlet*, to be fitted up as her summer residence, and had engaged him as her head dairyman.

A letter was at once dispatched, informing Madame Lochwalder of her new relatives.

Annette tried her best to get possession of this letter; but Margaret carried it to the post-office and mailed it with her own hands, and all Annette could do was to write a letter of explanation, which she sent by the same mail to her uncle, who was really the son of Madame Lochwalder.

"I have ascertained," she wrote, "that my employer is the son of your Uncle Jacob, who ran away to America so long ago. They have grand notions that Jacob was a nobleman in disguise, which will all be disappointed when they come to see you, with me, as they intend to do. They are wealthy people; and, though they will drop you all, as if you were hot coals, when they see how poor you are, still they will doubtless leave us the richer for their visit, if only to bribe us not to follow them to America, and disgrace them by proclaiming our relationship. Much can be gained from them, if we only manage well our opportunities. I enclose an answer to a letter which grandmother will receive from these people. I have written as I thought was best. It is well that grandmother cannot write, or she would spoil everything with her goodness of heart. Leave the matter to me. She must not expect any real kindness from these new relatives; they will despise us, and be ashamed of us."

It had first occurred to Annette to tell her uncle the truth, and admit that she was playing a clever deception for their own benefit; but on reflection she was sure that her family were too honest to join her in such a plot, and that even if they had been so unprincipled as to be willing to play their parts, they would be more naturally carried out, and with less risk of detection, if they really believed in the relationship. Madame Lochwalder, it happened, had a brother who had emigrated long before this to America, and this circumstance aided in carrying out her scheme.

The letter which she had enclosed in her own, and had sent to Switzerland, came back to Margaret in due time.

It read as follows:—

"Zermatt, April.

"My Dear Grand-Niece,—I am rejoiced to find you, after all these years. I have long felt that my brother must have died, since I no longer heard from him. It is strange that his son did not receive my letters. I am glad that you are coming to Switzerland. You will find your relatives glad to welcome you. Perhaps we shall induce you to remain with us. I long ago decided that if I could ever discover my brother's descendants I would share with them my earthly possessions while I live, and leave them my little estate when I die. I am an old woman, and cannot live many years longer. I trust you will come very soon, to

"Your affectionate aunt,
"MARGARET LOCHWALDER."

This letter decided them all, or would have decided them, if there had been any hesitation about the journey to Switzerland.

From this time forward everything favored the trip. Cecilia Boylston, a former Vassar girl, who had studied music in Germany after her graduation, and had taught in Boston since her return, had decided, previously to the events just related, to attend the Wagnerian festival to be celebrated that summer at Baireuth. She was readily persuaded that to go *via* Switzerland was really the most direct route, and gladly joined the party. Grandpa Houghton renewed his youth, and laid in a small library of Alpine literature to be read during the voyage, including all the guide-books on Switzerland, from Wagner to Murray, and accounts of the travels of noted mountaineers. (As these were principally in German, he trusted to having them translated by Margaret.) Several volumes of the Alpine Journal with the doings of the English Alpine Club, Mr. Whymper's account of his long-continued siege of the Matterhorn, Professor Tyndall's "Scrambles," Agassiz for geology, and Ruskin for art, with many other books, were added to the collection.

Besides the library, he purchased a large stock of articles likely to serve him in the Alps. No prospective bride ever enjoyed the shopping necessary for the preparation of her *trousseau* more than Judge Houghton the buying of his mountain outfit. There was a Kodak camera and other photographing appliances, an Arctic sleeping-bag, a spirit-lamp, and (though he was politically and practically a prohibitionist) a flask of spirits, a rifle for shooting chamois, remedies for chilblains, blue-glass spectacles against snow glare, and ice-spurs to steady his footsteps. That he did not make himself as ridiculous an object as Daudet's Tartarin, was simply owing to the fact that he proposed purchasing his alpenstock, pickaxe, rope, lantern, etc., in Geneva. The books were packed in a steamer trunk and slipped under Judge Houghton's berth, for ready reference; but stormy weather kept him uncomfortable, and the trunk was not once opened during the voyage.

GRANDFATHER HOUGHTON IN ALPINE COSTUME.

Grandma Houghton, relying on Margaret's care, awoke to a mild interest in the expedition, and knitted her husband a pair of very warm mittens. She also sent his overcoat to the tailor's, to be faced with fur; exhumed from the camphor-chest an ancient cap with ear-tabs, and packed away his gentlemanly beaver, lest, if he had it with him, he might be tempted to wear it in ascending Mont Blanc. The result of this wifely care was that Judge Houghton wore his mountain cap on a warm Sunday in Paris, and was the observed of all observers.

The party made a brief visit in Paris, but, on a bright day in early June, left the city by the Orleans Railroad, *via* Dijon and Macon, for Geneva. Margaret found this city disappointing, but Lake Leman, or as it is more often called, the Lake of Geneva, was very beautiful.

"It was Goethe who first said that lakes are the eyes of the landscape; and as our glance, perusing the living traits of a man, is never satisfied till it reaches his eye, so, on the earth, we seek after water, and are not quite content till our attention, long vagrant, rests in peace upon it." Lake Leman is the largest of the Swiss lakes. It has been said of it that, though it lacks the grandeur and sublimity of Lucerne and Thun, and the marvellous color of the Italian lakes, for bright, laughing beauty it is pre-eminent.

Margaret would gladly have taken the train for the south of Switzerland, but while they were in this region her grandfather insisted on making the tour of the lake, and, before doing this, in going through the city in true traveller's style. It would make a paragraph for his proposed lecture in Chickering Hall; and Margaret found, during the summer, that much was to be sacrificed for this famous lecture.

She went patiently with him as he made his visits to the watch manufactories, and took copious notes for his lecture, both from actual observation and from printed authorities. She would read these aloud in the evening, and Judge Houghton would express his opinion.

"Excellent, excellent!" the old gentleman would comment, after such a reading. "That is just what the members of the Geographical Society will want to hear. Copy it neatly for me, my dear. I only wish I had brought my typewriter."

Their first view of Mont Blanc was obtained at Geneva, with the lake in the foreground. "How delightful it will be to make the ascent!" Judge Houghton remarked cheerfully. "It does not look nearly as difficult as I imagined."

But when he took Turner's "Liber Studiorum" from his steamer-trunk that evening, and studied the etching of the *Mer de Glace*, in which the savage character of the glacier is greatly exaggerated, and the great causeway is represented as a chaos of jagged splinters, he shook his head doubtfully, and hoped there was some easier way. His assurance increased as he bought his alpenstock the next day.

"MER DE GLACE," MONT BLANC.

It was topped with a chamois' horn, and pointed with a sharp iron ferrule. "We will have the names of the mountains you have ascended branded on the staff free of charge, on your return from your tour," the tradesman kindly offered.

Judge Houghton reflected a moment. "We are not certain to come back this way," he said. "I think it would do just as well to mark the names of the peaks I intend to ascend, now."

"As you please, sir. What mountains do you wish? The Rigi, I presume. That is quite easy to climb. And the Brunig."

"Certainly, certainly. But I want some of the celebrated peaks too,— the Jungfrau, and Mont Blanc, and the Matterhorn."

"Those are rather difficult to ascend," the tradesman replied with a smile.

"'What man has done man can do,'" Judge Houghton remarked cheerfully and confidently, with refreshing ignorance of what he was attempting.

At the Museum of Natural History the stuffed chamois excited his enthusiasm, and he inquired for the taxidermist who had mounted them. "I shall send him all the game I shoot," he remarked, as he made a note of the address. "I think I shall make a present of the collection to the New York Museum of Natural History."

ALICE NEWTON.

"Suppose it should not prove to be a very large collection, grandpa?" Margaret suggested mischievously, but was glad that the old man did not hear her. It was at the Archæological Museum, and while examining an ancient boat, one of the relics of the lacrustine period, that Margaret met another Vassar girl, Alice Newton, an old friend of Cecilia's, and now a missionary to Bulgaria. She had come to Switzerland to meet her mother, who had been recently left a widow, and, having no other near ties in America, had decided to join her missionary daughter, and aid her as a volunteer.

Alice was delighted to meet Margaret, for Vassar is a pass-word among its alumnæ. "I have been living for a week in Geneva with mother," she said. "I have a little vacation, and I do not want to hurry her to Bulgaria. I shall return by way of the Danube. I hope our routes lie the same way."

THE GIRL IN THE HADING VEIL.

"Unfortunately," said Margaret, "we travel in quite another direction."

"But it happens very nicely for me," Cecilia explained, "since I must part from Margaret and the rest of the party when they turn southward. I shall be very glad to have you as a travelling companion. We can journey together as far as Bavaria."

"And we are not going south immediately," Grandfather Houghton remarked confidently. "It would be a shame to give less than a fortnight to this lovely lake and the interesting towns on its shores. So there is no need of talking about our ways separating, at present."

Grandfather Houghton liked young girls. He enjoyed Cecilia's society, and Alice's calm, placid face had made a pleasant impression upon him. "It's a pity that you are not at our hotel," he added. "There are plenty of people there, but no one that the girls seem to take to particularly. Though that pretty girl in the Hading veil strikes me as rather nice."

Margaret laughed merrily. "Grandpa is so impressionable," she explained. "The girl in the veil is pretty, but that is all there is to her,—and she has the most dreadful mother. They are Americans living abroad on their income. The father, I infer from the mother's interest in business, is no more."

"How does the widow show her business faculty?" Alice asked.

"She takes the American papers and reads the stock quotations while she eats her breakfast, interrupting whatever conversation may be going on by such exclamations as

CALUMET AND HECLA.

'Calumet and Hecla's up! Now, Betty, you can buy that embroidered muslin you wanted.' Or, 'The land! Betty. Calumet and Hecla's down. I'm sorry I ordered that music-box.'"

"You describe her very well," said the Judge. "She's something of a terror, but she's better than the men. She's American, at least, and I can understand her; but my Lord Highnose and I haven't a notion in common."

"Is that a real name?" Alice asked, much amused.

"Only a nickname that Margaret has given him. We thought he was an Englishman; for he is deplorably ignorant in regard to America, and seems to take a positive pride in displaying his ignorance. He asked me, for instance, if Calumet and Hecla were two noted race-horses, or Mississippi steamers! And then it came out that he hadn't the excuse of being an Englishman; for he said that he had been absent from the States so long that he had rather lost the run of affairs. When I told him that Calumet and Hecla was a favorite kind of stock in the market, and that the lady was interested in Wall Street bulls, he said, 'Ah, yes! a lady drover and cattle raiser. How very extraordinary!' I am glad that we are soon to see the last of these people."

The girls assented, and Alice asked if there was really no one at their hotel who was more interesting.

"Yes," replied the Judge; "there is a young scientist, whom I rather like. He is on his way to make the ascension of the Jungfrau, and intends to scramble about in the Oberland all summer. He's a Harvard student, and his name is Livingston Walker; and — 'Speak of an angel' — the young fellow is entering the Museum now. May I present him?"

LORD HIGHNOSE.

The young man proved to be intelligent and courteous. Their conversation drifted to the work and fame of Professor Agassiz.

"I am glad to find," said Judge Houghton, "that at least one American scientist is recognized here in Europe. I have found his name several times in the Museum."

"The Genevese would probably claim him as a Swiss scientist," the young man replied. "He was born at Motier, in the Canton de Vaud, not very far from us, and educated in Swiss and German universities. You know his first work that attracted attention was on the fresh-water fishes of Europe; and I can imagine him as a boy an enthusiastic angler in the Swiss lakes. Later, he extended his researches to fossil fishes. He became Professor of Natural History at Neuchatel, on the lake of the same name, north of us. I have just returned from a visit to the city. I found the museum rich with collections which he had named and classified, and the library, with learned treatises from his pen. Yes; the Swiss can certainly claim him, though we have also the right to do so. At present, I am making an Agassiz pilgrimage, following his footsteps everywhere in Switzerland. It is a labor of love, in every way, I assure you."

"Quite an idea," exclaimed the enthusiastic Judge. "Let us, also, visit Neuchatel, and make an Agassiz pilgrimage."

Margaret bit her lip. "As we return, grandpa, if you like; but just now, please remember how impatient I am to reach Zermatt."

"True, true," assented the old gentleman. "It will do just as well to go there when we come back. And meantime, I have his 'Researches on Glaciers' in my trunk, which you may read to me in the evening; and perhaps I can bring a part of it into my lecture."

"If you are interested in glaciers," said Mr. Walker, "we may possibly meet on the great glacier of the Aar. I shall be making studies next month in the vicinity of Agassiz's cabin, which he jokingly called the Hotel Neuchatelois. I shall be happy if I can be of any service."

MR. WALKER.

Margaret bowed. She did not care to have her grandfather's interest drawn from Zermatt, and she asked if the glaciers at the foot of the Matterhorn were not as accessible as those of the Aar. "More so," replied the young man; "and Agassiz has mapped them. I mean to work around to that point before the end of the season; and somewhere, I trust, I may have the pleasure of meeting you again."

The wish was emphatically echoed by the Judge, and the young man withdrew, the others passing into the library founded by Bonnivard.

"He was the true prisoner of Chillon," Alice said, "of whom Byron had not heard when he wrote his poem."

THE HOTEL NEUCHATELOIS.

"Bonnivard?" remarked the Judge questioningly. "I don't quite recollect his history."

"He was the Prior of St. Victor, you know," Alice replied. "He was a patriot, too, and greatly opposed to the usurpation of the Duke of Savoy; and the duke had him carried to Chillon, and kept there as a prisoner for six years."

"How did he ever get out?"

"In 1536, the people of Geneva assaulted the castle from the lake, and rescued him."

"It seems to me they took a long enough time to make up their minds to do it." This from Margaret.

"That reminds me," said the Judge, "that we must certainly visit Chillon; and I think it would be pleasanter to go by the lake. I wonder if there is not some pleasant little place at the other end of Lake Leman which we could make our headquarters, and then take excursions from it to Vevy, Clarens, and other interesting points."

"Glion is just the spot," replied Alice. "Mamma and I are going there. The Pension Victoria has been recommended to us as a homelike, charming little hotel, situated on a commanding height, and giving one beautiful views in every direction."

THE PRISONER OF CHILLON.

"A good place to practise mountain climbing, eh! Then, to Glion let us all go. A few days more will suffice for Geneva; then farewell to Calumet and Hecla."

The morning of the next day Judge Houghton spent in looking up a music-box. He succeeded in finding a fine one, which played the air of a song by Grieg, beginning, —

"The winter may perish, the spring pass away,"

which Cecilia sang charmingly, and which was a prime favorite with the Judge.

After the music-box was purchased, it proved quite an elephant. Judge Houghton would not hear to its being packed in the trunk, and left to the tender mercies of baggage-smashers; and it was accordingly wrapped in Cecilia's water-proof, and carried by a shawl-strap. As they walked back to the hotel from the shop, a slight jar set the mechanism in motion; and people whom they met or passed turned to wonder what was the source of the fairy music. Among these was Mr. Walker, who smilingly asked, "Is this the Banbury Cross lady, of whom it was said that 'she shall have music wherever she goes'?"

"It is disagreeable, is it not, to be made so conspicuous?" Margaret remarked, as Mr. Walker relieved her of the burden.

"It is a familiar air," replied the young man, "and the words set to it are very beautiful."

"I think them very sentimental," Margaret replied, with a toss of her head. "I thought, last night, while Cecilia was singing them with so much apparent feeling, that it was all great nonsense."

"So," thought Mr. Walker, "our young lady is not the least bit romantic. Well, I like her all the better for it."

The Judge, however, took up the cudgels in favor of the little love-song. "Mr. Walker must hear Cecilia sing it," he said. "Mrs. and Miss Newton are to dine with us this evening; and after dinner, if no one else has taken possession of the little music-room, perhaps Mr. Walker will join us there, and we will have some music."

Mr. Walker responded gratefully to the Judge's invitation, and fortune favored them, in providing some fireworks in the public gardens, to which the other guests of the hotel gave their countenance. The hotel parlors were deserted, and the Judge escorted Cecilia to the piano.

From singing, they fell to chatting of the great names connected with Geneva, of Rousseau, of Voltaire, and Calvin.

Mrs. Newton, who had a refined, serious face, a typical mother, as Margaret expressed it, was a clergyman's wife, who delighted in her daughter's work. She joined in the conversation enthusiastically and intelligently.

"There are many interesting lives that have been influenced by these mountains," she said; "but to me, Calvin is far the strongest. You know he fled to Switzerland when he embraced Protestantism. It was from Basel that he wrote his famous preface to Francis I., which has been called one of the most memorable documents of the Reformation, 'from its intensity of feeling, its indignant remonstrance, and its pathetic and powerful eloquence.'"

"I wonder whether Calvin was really influenced by the 'mountain gloom,' of which Ruskin has so much to say," Cecilia remarked.

"I think not," Alice replied; "for his life in Switzerland was spent chiefly here in Geneva, where nature has a very cheerful aspect; but he may well have drawn his dogmas in relation to 'Irresistible Grace' and the eternal decrees of God from the irresistible onward sweep of the glaciers and the stability of the everlasting hills."

"I am not drawn to Calvin as I am to Luther," Cecilia remarked musingly. "He seems to me the Torquemada of the Protestant Church."

Judge Houghton began to fear that their missionary friends would prove rather heavy companions, but Alice considerately changed the subject. She had that valuable quality which we call tact, the power of adapting herself to her friends, and of making herself beloved by widely differing individuals. "What led you to be so greatly interested in Agassiz?" she asked of Mr. Walker. "You are certainly too young to have been one of his pupils, even at Penikese."

"It is the regret of my life that I came into the world too late to be his pupil," replied the young man. "But I had the privilege of studying his wonderful collection at Cambridge, and I feel that in that he has left me a rich personal legacy."

"You are a geologist?"

"I am fond of the natural sciences, but they are only a luxury for me. My profession is to be that of a civil engineer; and part of my business here in Switzerland is to study the passes and the railroad engineering of the Alps, in the hope that I may some time improve upon them in our Rocky Mountains."

The return of "Calumet and Hecla" from viewing the fireworks reminded Mrs. Newton of the lateness of the hour, and she and Alice took their leave, Mr. Walker escorting them to their *pension*.

During the few days that they remained in Geneva, some playful chance was continually throwing the young people together. Did they walk in the gardens, Mr. Walker was sure to appear near the statue of Rousseau. At church, on Sabbath, the sexton oddly showed him into the pew behind them. In the photograph shops, Mr. Walker turned the portfolios. Did they take a drive, Mr. Walker cantered up beside them in the most off-hand manner.

"This is getting monotonous," Margaret said to Cecilia, on their last evening in Geneva, as the waiter handed them Mr. Walker's card; " but there is one comfort, there will be an entire change of *dramatis personæ* at Glion."

Mrs. Newton and Alice dropped in a little later, and the evening was one of the pleasantest which they had passed in Geneva. Was it the sense of coming relief which made Margaret more than usually gay and sparkling, and really courteous to the "Monotonous Walker"? If so, she must have been a trifle nonplussed when he asked, as he took his leave, if he might be permitted to call on them at Glion, on his way to the Oberland? The request was addressed to Margaret; but apparently she did not hear it, and the Judge filled in the awkward pause with a profuse welcome, and Mrs. Newton, in response to a gentle pressure from Alice's hand, added a gracious assurance of favor.

CHAPTER IV.

THE COUNTESS.

> "Glion? Ah, twenty years, it cuts
>   All meaning from a name!
> White houses prank where once were huts;
>   Glion, but not the same.
>
> "And yet I know not. All unchanged
>   The turf, the pines, the sky!
> The hills in their old order ranged!
>   The lake with Chillon by!"
>   MATTHEW ARNOLD.

OUR travellers were enchanted with their first view of Glion, the picturesque villas and hotels gleaming on the green mountain side. A funicular railway carried the guests of the hotels up the steep slope to their destination; but the Judge preferred to begin his mountaineering by walking to the hotel, and Margaret accompanied him, the rest mounting by rail. It was a longer walk than they had counted on, and the Judge's bandanna came out frequently to wipe his perspiring brow; but the view was superb, and refreshed their spirits when they paused to rest. There was the Castle of Chillon at their feet, and the sapphire lake dimpling in the breeze, and flecked with white sails, the nestling towns and villages on the shore — Montreux, Clarens, and Vevey — all plainly visible. In the direction of the Gorge of the Rhone, the Dent du Midi and the Alps of the Valais lifted white fingers of snow, as one traveller has so well said, "As though the hills themselves were holding up their hands in everlasting homage."

Margaret stood afterwards before many scenes surpassing this in grandeur, but never felt herself more thrilled by pure beauty than now. The Judge was exhilarated, and as happy as a child. "If all Alpine climbing is as easy as this—," he remarked; "but then, of course, it can't be."

At a sudden turn they came upon a little old woman resting by the roadside. She was dressed plainly, but her garments were of rich material, and she was presided over by a servant in livery, who held a parasol over her, and fanned her assiduously.

"Enough, animal!" she cried spitefully, in French. "You will give me the consumption, with such a current of air. You are worse than an Alpine hurricane, you blacksmith's bellows. Put away that fan, and hand me my lorgnette. Let me see what manner of creatures these are."

THE COUNTESS.

The footman obediently folded the fan and handed his mistress her eye-glasses, and the little woman coolly submitted the Judge and Margaret to a broadside of scrutiny. "A grizzly bear," she remarked, still speaking in French; "an American bear. I know the species. Hold, he has with him a little savagess. Their air is amiable. I will speak to them." And dropping her eye-glass and totally changing her manner, she addressed them in odd English, with a slightly foreign accent.

"Make your father to be seated, my dear young lady. He has ze air to be fatigued. My servant will bring him a glass of water from ze cascade yonder. Animal, approach ze water." (This to the footman, who incontinently fled to execute the errand.)

Margaret, who had heard and comprehended her soliloquy, would have declined her courtesy and proceeded; but Judge Houghton did not understand French, and, as he was really weary, eagerly availed himself of the proffered civilities, seating himself on the stone parapet beside the stranger, and mopping his glowing countenance.

"I am very glad to meet any one who speaks English, ma'am," he said, by way of keeping up the conversation; for Margaret stood at a little distance, apparently absorbed in the view.

"You are zen English?" asked the lady.

"American, ma'am; American. Allow me to introduce myself. Judge Jonah Houghton of New York." He paused, but the lady did not respond to the introduction by giving her own name, and he continued, "Travelling with my granddaughter. You, I judge, are a foreigner, ma'am; though you speak English like a native." For the moment, Judge Houghton forgot that here in Europe he was the foreigner; but the lady understood him, and bowed politely, though an amused smile twitched her thin lips, while the Judge proceeded serenely, "It is really remarkable, but you are the first foreigner we've really met, — socially, I mean. I don't count storekeepers. Switzerland seems to be full of Americans. At least, the hotels are. Margaret and I are sick of them. Americans are all very well in America; but one can see plenty of them at home; one doesn't come abroad to see them. I mean no disparagement of my own country people when I say it. They may be a great deal more enlightened than foreigners; but when we come abroad we come to study foreigners, their ways and their manners, even if they are not up to our own, and that is why I am so glad to make your acquaintance, ma'am."

Margaret felt that the conversation needed interruption, and, stepping forward, remarked on the beauty of the view. "It is lufly, very lufly," said the lady. "I know it well; for I have been here before. Eighteen years ago since I was in Switzerland. You can well comprehend zat it has changed. Zere was no funicular railway zen. We rode to ze top in ze omnibus, or we walked. I always walked. So, to revive ze old time, I have walked to-day. But alas! I have changed also. I am not so spry as once. Better I had gone in ze wagon of ze train, with Lajos, for it has proved a great waste of perspiration. Come, Konrad. I have reposed myself, and I will not make zese kind people to wait longer. *En route!*"

LAJOS.

The footman gave her his arm, and they all walked on together. It seemed odd to Margaret to hear her address the servant as Konrad; she had called him "animal" so often, that it almost seemed that this must be his Christian name.

But though violent of temper, this strange old woman was not uninteresting, and Margaret admired her intelligence. She quoted from Rousseau, and Byron's lines on Clarens, as the Judge pointed out the town.

"Have you anyzing so beautiful as zat by an American writer?" she asked.

"I think Aldrich's 'Alpine Picture' more beautiful," Margaret replied. And, as the lady knew of neither the poet nor the poem, she repeated it for her.

"Stand here and look, and softly hold your breath,
Lest the vast avalanche come crashing down!
How many miles away is yonder town,
Set flower-wise in the valley? Far beneath,
A scimitar half drawn from out its sheath,
The river curves through meadows newly mown.
The ancient water-courses all are strown
With drifts of snow, fantastic wreath on wreath.
And peak on peak against the turquoise blue,
The Alps like towering campanilis stand,
Wondrous, with pinnacles of frozen rain,
Silvery, crystal, like the prism in hue.
O tell me, love, if this be Switzerland,
Or is it but the frost-work on the pane?"

The little woman listened attentively, and then remarked half to herself, "You are fond of poetry. Ah! yes; you are at ze romantic period. You have perhaps eighteen years. It must be passed through. It does not always make harm. I am not of zose who would repress it. One might as well try to repress ze chicken-pox. It can be done, but it is bad for ze liver; and when ze eruption of poetry is driven in, it is bad for ze heart. Much better you go through wiz zese infantile diseases at ze proper time. Lajos has never had ze measles. I tremble for him if he should contract zem now. He has never had a romance in his youth. Zink of the virulence wiz which it may attack him in his manhood. You see, my dear, Lajos is my nephew; zat is, not my true nephew. He is ze nephew to my husband, who is dead. We are all zere is to each other. He is so devoted to me, he will do anyzing I ask of him. He would have climbed ze mountain wiz me; but I said, 'Lajos, you have had enough of mountains.' He joined the Russian army, and went over ze Balkans with General Skobeleff. He was wounded in ze leg, and nursed in a hospital of ze Red Cross, by some Americans. I have felt kindly to Americans ever since. But all ze same, he cannot walk well, or dance. It is hard for him. He has changed since zat campaign. He is not ze same lively, gay of heart boy as once."

By the time that they had climbed the mountain and reached the hotel, they all felt very well acquainted.

"I shall see you again, my dear," said the little woman as they separated at the door, and she took the arm of a hollow-cheeked, grave man, with an immense mustache. It was difficult to imagine that this was her "boy" Lajos; but he led the strange little lady toward Alice, saying as he did so, "I wish, my aunt, to present you to Mrs. Newton, and to Miss Newton, to whose kind care while in the hospital I believe I owe my life."

"He is the Count Krajova," Alice explained afterwards. "He was taken prisoner by the Turks toward the last of the war, spared on account of his high rank, and sent to Lady Strangford's hospital, where I was assisting. I helped nurse him until the Russians took Kezanlik, when he was transferred to the Red Cross hospital. He recognized me in the cars as we rode up, and came over to see us at once, and inquired for the mission and the girls' school, of which I had told him when he asked how it happened that an American girl had drifted so far from home."

"I remember your writing about him," said Mrs. Newton.

"Did I mention him?" Alice asked. "That is odd, for he was with us only a short time; but he was very gentlemanly. He was more than that, he was heroic in his patient endurance."

"At last," said Judge Houghton, as he inscribed his name in the hotel register, and tried in vain to make out those of the Austrians which preceded it, "at last we have escaped from our co-patriots." But as he spoke, a girlish voice from the reading-room exclaimed in triumph, "Ma, Ma; we can stay in Switzerland all summer. Calumet and Hecla is up!"

The Judge started. "They are some American ladies," said the clerk, "who arrived to-day from Geneva. They came by rail. Would you like to meet them?"

"Far be it from me," replied the Judge; and he impressed on the mind of the clerk their especial desire during their stay to avoid the society of all Americans.

"I'll do the best I can, sir," replied the obliging clerk; "but we are quite overrun with them this summer."

The Judge was weary, and retired early; but as the girls sat by their open window looking down at the rakish lateen sails of the fishing craft on the lake, a maid appeared, dressed in the pretty costume of the country, and bringing an invitation from the Countess Krajova inviting the American party to drive with her to Vevey the next day.

The invitation was accepted, and the party made the excursion in two carriages.

It was a day to be marked with a white stone, as nearly all days are in the beautiful Pays de Vaud. They drove through the lovely town of Montreux, through woods and vineyards, over streams and along the borders of the lake, catching glimpses of the Plejaden, the Moleson, and the Cubli mountains, with new combinations of the familiar Dent de Jaman and Dent du Midi.

"CALUMET AND HECLA IS UP!"

"It is one pity it is not ze autumn," said the countess; "for zen we could see ze Fête of ze Abbaye des Vignerons."

"What is that?" asked the Judge. "Some church festival?"

"On ze contrarie," replied the lady, "it is one survive of ze Paganism celebrate by ze vine-dresser in honor of Bacchus. It is now twenty years zat I have not seen it. Such so great pleasure! It was worth to be one Pagan. Ze town was so full of ze spectator from effery country of Europe zat it was unpossible zere could come more. Ze window, ze balcony, ze roof, even ze tree, was rent for a price to preak ze heart. Only ze American could afford ze best place. Ze aristocracy of Europe content himself to view zat processions from ze barn, from ze wagon of hay. I have accommodate myself, wiz ze Countess Esterhazy, on ze roof of a smissy [smithy]. We could not else. We were bake by ze sun, and robe was decorate wiz ze tar and ze cinder, — but all zat signify to us nossing, we have excellent view to ze procession."

"They will manage it better this year, aunt," said Lajos. "Parisian artists are designing the tableaux, which are to be superb; and the public will be provided for more commodiously."

"It cannot be more beautiful as then," said the countess. "Do you know if ze Goddess of Spring shall be ze same pretty peasant girl of Clarens who took ze part when I was here? Ze Prince of Metternich made her a present of a pracelet of diamond."

PEASANT WAITRESS.

"Your peasant beauty must be a buxom dame by this time, aunt. You forget the changes that Time works."

"Ah! malicious one; it is true. You could not believe I was beautiful also. I wore a green satin pelisse; and my friend Margaret du Fais, one of pink, garnished wiz ze down of swan. We were ze toast of ze gentlemen; and she is dead, ze beloved one."

THE DENT DU MIDI FROM ABOVE THE LAKE OF GENEVA.

"But the spectacle, aunt," said Lajos, anxious to lead her thoughts from sad personal recollections.

"Ah! ze spectacle was magnifique. I can see it all. First ze train of ze Goddess of Spring; ze gardeners and gardencresses wiz zare tools, ze shepherd and shepherdesses wiz zare sheeps, ze herdsmen wiz zare cattles, all shouting ze Ranz des vaches. Oh! it was heavenly beautiful! And ze Goddess of Summer, in a wagon ornamented of corns. Zen come some children carrying a cage of bees, singing alouds. And ze laborer of autumn; ze haymakers wiz zare pitchforks, ze mowers wiz *seys*, ze gleaners wiz sheafs, and ze vintagers wiz ze cluster of grape, ze faun, ze Bacchante, and ze people mythologique, dressed in skin of leopard and garlands, dancing wiz great leaps. Ze pipes, ze flutes, ze kettledrum, ze fiddle, making music forte fortissimo!"

The countess' description was so spirited that the volatile Judge was greatly interested. "Let us remain until the fête," he exclaimed, forgetful of all other plans.

"Rather, let us try to meet here again in the autumn," suggested Lajos.

"Excellent, excellent," said the countess. "It is fully three months until ze time of ze fête. One could not exist at Glion so long. It would be a century of *ennui*."

"And even if it were the most interesting place in the world," added Margaret, "we would all be very tired of one another."

"You would all weary of me," replied the countess; "but Lajos is an angel. If it were not so he could not have borne wiz me all zese years." It was plainly to be seen that the young man was her idol, and that she desired to have him admired by all, and especially by Margaret, to whom she seemed to have taken a strong liking. Margaret was gratified by her attentions; for she recognized the compliment which they implied, coming as they did from a lady of rank, and Margaret was not insensible to social distinction; but she did not reciprocate the affection offered her, for, in spite of her freakish kindness to Margaret and her doting fondness for her nephew, the countess was not an amiable woman. She did not scruple to fly into a rage over very little matters with her domestics, and to berate them in what seemed to Margaret a very unladylike manner. On unpacking the lunch hamper for their picnic on the border of the lake, it was discovered that one of the Bohemian glass decanters was broken, and the angry countess did not hesitate to give the unoffending maid who informed her of the fact a smart slap on the face. Lajos presently gave the girl a fee; but the revengeful look did not die out with the gift, and though the countess chatted merrily as though nothing unusual had happened, a restraint seemed to have fallen upon the spirits of the party.

When the wine was passed, and the girls declined it, the countess seemed to think that they did so because they feared that, one bottle having been broken, there would not be a sufficient quantity for all.

It was with great difficulty that Margaret explained to her that American girls did not drink wine.

"So!" she exclaimed. "But you, Miss Newton, you have in Europe been long enough to learn our customs." When Alice, also, resolutely begged to be excused, the countess exclaimed spitefully, "You are one leetle frog!"

They drove back to the hotel by a different route, with the sunset flushing the lake. Lajos, who rode with the young ladies, trolled German student songs in a rich baritone voice, and the young ladies responded with Vassar glees. "If one might ride and sing forever," said the young man in an impersonal manner, but directing his gaze at Alice. "But, alas, my aunt leaves Glion soon, for Austria, and I must accompany her." The words did not compromise him, but the tone said, "I am bound hand and foot to that woman; and no one knows what slavery it is."

The next day was the Sabbath, and the Americans attended service at the little church of Montreux.

"'I will lift up mine eyes unto the hills,'" Cecilia said softly, as they came out of the church door, and saw the beautiful Dent du Midi gleaming white in the distance. Lajos was on the terrace, waiting to walk home with them, and apparently not minding the climb at all.

"What a wonderful country this beautiful Pays de Vaud is!" Alice remarked softly. "I do not wonder that Agassiz grew near to Nature's heart here. Do you remember Longfellow's poem to him on his fiftieth birthday? I forgot to ask Mr. Walker if he was familiar with it; but of course he is."

"Can you repeat it?" Margaret asked; and as they climbed the hill together, Margaret repeated, —

> "It was fifty years ago,
>   In the pleasant month of May,
>   In the beautiful Pays du Vaud,
>   A child in its cradle lay.
>
> "And Nature, the old nurse, took
>   The child upon her keee,
>   Saying, 'Here is a story book
>   Thy Father has written for thee.
>
> "'Come, wander with me,' she said,
>   'Into regions yet untrod,
>   And read what is still unread
>   In the manuscripts of God.'
>
> "And he wandered away and away,
>   With Nature, the dear old nurse,
>   Who sang to him every day
>   The rhymes of the universe.
>
> "And whenever the way seemed long,
>   Or his heart began to fail,
>   She would sing a more wonderful song,
>   Or tell a more marvellous tale.

"And at times he hears in his dreams
  The Ranz des Vaches of old,
And the rush of mountain streams
  From glaciers clear and cold.

"And the mother at home says, 'Hark,
  For his voice I listen and yearn;
It is growing late and dark,
  And my boy does not return.'"

"It is indeed beautiful," said Lajós. "And you say that this was written to a Swiss scientist by your great poet Longfellow? But who is the Mr. Walker of whom you just spoke?"

"He is a young engineer whom we met in Geneva," Alice replied. "He has come to Switzerland to study the passes; but he is also much interested in Agassiz."

"Napoleon was the great engineer of Switzerland," Lajos asserted. "He should study the campaigns of Napoleon. I have myself studied engineering. That was a heavy bit of it we did in crossing the Balkans. I consider Prince Tserteleff one of our greatest military engineers. I helped him make the Hainkoi Pass practicable. Alas! there is no more military engineering for me." And he leaned heavily on his cane.

"I would like, however, to meet this friend of yours, and talk over engineering with him. I used to think of following up Napoleon's military works in the Alps, and making a thorough study of them; but I fear I shall never do even that."

"Mr. Walker may come to Glion," Alice replied; "and if so, I have no doubt that he will consider it a privilege to meet you. It is very kind of you to propose it. I am sure he deserves your interest."

Both Lajos and Margaret regarded Alice keenly, and each wondered how far she might be interested in the career of this young engineer; but Alice, utterly unconscious of their thought, and with nothing but simple friendship in her heart for Mr. Walker, continued the conversation. "Could you not go over most of the passes in a carriage?" she asked.

"The Simplon, certainly," he replied; "and doubtless the others. But one could not study them to the best advantage in that way; and I wanted to write an exhaustive work on the subject."

"Perhaps Mr. Walker could aid you in your observations, and enable you to carry out your plan. He may be able to be really useful to you; and if so, I shall be very glad."

"At all events, let me know when he appears," said Lajos.

That evening Konrad appeared with another invitation from Madame. This time it was for a social game of cards. The girls looked at each other in dismay.

"Tell her," said Margaret, impulsively, "that we don't play cards Sunday night."

"Wait a moment, dear," said Alice. "As mamma is our *chaperone*, would it not be better for her to send a note of explanation?"

THE COUNTESS ENTHRONED.

This was accordingly done, the countess immediately deferring the party until the next evening.

She was enthroned in a high-backed chair as they entered, industriously reading from a French novel; but she dropped the book, and greeted them vivaciously.

"We will play Lansquenet," she said; "for so we shall not limit ourself at four." And she led the way to a table on which she had already distributed the cards. Margaret was thunderstruck to see a roll of silver pieces at each place.

"We are not to play for money!" she exclaimed. "I thought that was against the law."

"It is against the law to keep a public gambling house," Lajos explained; "but the police do not trouble themselves with an innocent little amusement like this. We never play for high stakes, and it adds a zest to the game."

"But we never play for money in America," Alice replied, laying down her cards.

"Avaricious one!" exclaimed the countess; "do you not see zat I have provide ze silver? You lose nossing. On contrary, you shall keep your gains."

"It is not that," Alice explained bravely. "It is the principle of the thing. We think it wrong."

The countess flushed angrily. "Bigote!" she exclaimed, turning abruptly from the table, and flouncing out of the room. Alice's eyes shone suspiciously, and Lajos gave her a quick glance of sympathy, but refrained from speaking to her, for he saw that a word now would unloose the tears. He rose at once, and, begging that they might be favored with some music, escorted Cecilia to the piano; and Cecilia played a merrier selection than was her wont, a Hungarian dance of Rubenstein's. The countess heard it, in the depths of her *boudoir*. It was one of her favorites, and she could not resist its contagion. She flew in, all animation, exclaiming, "We dance, we dance," and, catching Margaret about the waist, spun her around the room until she was breathless.

When the dance ceased, Margaret noticed that Lajos had led Alice out upon the balcony, and was talking with her in the moonlight. "You are right," he said. "I have seen the evils of gaming in the army. You have taught me a lesson. I will never play for money again."

Konrad came in with refreshments, — little cakes, and glasses of "limonad." The countess had evidently regarded the prejudices of her guests, though she herself declined the beverage, declaring it made her shiver to think of it.

So a week passed, rendering them all better and better acquainted with each other's good qualities and faults; for the latter come out with even more startling distinctness during travel than at home.

Annette was the only one of the party who had not yet seen the Countess Krajova; but the name and title was unfamiliar to her, and she had as yet no suspicion that the baroness whom she had known years ago might in the interval have married a count, and be known by her husband's name and title.

The culmination of their intercourse occurred a few days after this. Alice and Margaret were sitting alone one afternoon, when Konrad came running to their room, exclaiming, "The countess! The countess! She has poisoned herself!"

"What? On purpose?" Alice asked.

"No. She have one dreadful headache, and she take some medicine. And now I tink she die."

"Where is Lajos?" asked Alice.

"I know not. He have depart."

"Then, run for a physician, and we will go to her meantime." Alice had had experience in the hospital; but Margaret was younger, and knew nothing of medicine. She followed Alice, feeling all the time as if she were in a dream. The countess lay upon a couch, her face distorted, her form bent, and her fingers contracted, as though suddenly frozen stiff in the midst of a convulsion.

Alice stepped quickly to the dressing-table. The vial labelled Nux Vomica from which she had taken the medicine stood uncorked, a teaspoon beside it.

"It is what you call homœopathic medicine," said the trembling maid. "That never hurt anybody."

Alice read the printed direction. "Mix four drops of the tincture in a third of a glass of water, and take one teaspoonful at each dose."

But the countess had taken one teaspoonful of the tincture, washing it down with a third of a glass of water.

"That make all the same, is it not?" asked the maid.

"Hardly," replied Alice. "It is deadly poison. She has taken enough to kill her. The antidote is tannic acid; and the pharmacist's is so far away that we can never get it here in time. We can only give an emetic. Quick! Get me some mustard and hot water."

The maid brought the mixture. "We can never make her take it," said Margaret. "Her teeth are ground tightly together. I believe she has lockjaw."

"The entomologist up-stairs must have chloroform," replied Alice. "Run and ask him for some. A sniff of it will make the muscles relax, and then she can open her mouth and take the medicine."

THE ENTOMOLOGIST RECEIVES THE APOLOGY.

Margaret sped up to the old entomologist's room, but he was away among the hills chasing Alpine butterflies. His door was locked, but she bethought her suddenly of Annette's skeleton key. Down-stairs again, to explain the matter to Annette, who opened the door with a triumphant manner which said plainly, "Now, you see, yourself, the good of having a brother who is a locksmith, and can commit burglary without a scruple, when it serves your purpose."

Margaret, having first carried down a bottle of glue, which would not have had a relaxing tendency, at last found the chloroform in the old gentleman's dressing-case. What a time they had afterwards, explaining the burglary to the deaf old entomologist, and how pleased he was that his chloroform had the desired effect! "And now," said Alice, "if I only had the tannic acid!"

Margaret's wits slowly came to her. "Alice, they use tannic acid in ink, do they not?"

"Yes; but combined with iron. Ink would not serve the purpose."

"I know it. But grandpa was complaining of the ink we have here, and bought some chemicals the other day, to make some for his precious lecture; and I am sure that he has not used them yet." And Margaret flew to her grandfather's room, returning with the tannic acid, and bringing Annette to assist. Annette, however, was of little service. "Hand me the smelling-salts," Alice had said. "Look on the dressing-table. You surely will find a vinaigrette."

Annette fumbled among the articles displayed on the dainty toilet-table, her gaze fixed on a well-known crest on the silver vinaigrette, — a mailed hand waving a firebrand.

"Quick, Annette; the vinaigrette! She is fainting," exclaimed Margaret. "You cannot find it? Why, girl! it is in your hand," Annette turned, and gave the countess one long, terrified stare. The features were unfamiliar, but years might have changed them. She dared not await her return to consciousness; and when Margaret, whose hand had been extended for the smelling-salts, looked up impatiently, Annette was gone. The girls continued their efforts until the arrival of the physician, who listened to what they had done, gave some remedies, and congratulated them warmly. "You have saved the lady's life," he said. "But for your prompt action, I should have arrived too late." Lajos, who entered at this moment, clasped Alice's hand. "This is like you," he said simply.

It was several days before the countess fully recovered; but, when told of what had happened, she perversely insisted on giving all the credit to Margaret. It was in vain that Margaret herself disclaimed the merit, explaining that she only followed Alice's directions, and that without her she would not have known what to do. The countess persisted in attributing Margaret's statement of the fact to her own modesty.

When Lajos rather indignantly urged that Alice's participation in the rescue should not be ignored, the countess grudgingly accorded her an expression of her gratitude. It was evident that she had contracted an unreasoning prejudice toward Alice and an equally unfounded fondness for Margaret. She could not bear, now, to allow a single day to pass without seeing her. She made her handsome presents, — an exquisitely embroidered Swiss muslin dress, and a pretty necklace of edelweiss blossom in frosted silver. Her manner softened appreciably. She had been very near death, and had felt the spray of that unknown sea upon her face. Her eyes assumed a wistful expression. They followed Margaret beseechingly. Her fondness wearied Margaret, who was not then as unselfish as she afterward became. It was not altogether pleasant to read continually to an invalid instead of roaming freely with the others. And when the countess was able to join them in their excursions it was just a little wearying to have her claw-like hand forever resting upon her arm, to adapt her steps to the cramped hobble of her companion, and to respond to her questions, while the Judge, tripping on in advance, laughed heartily at Cecilia's witticisms, which Margaret could not hear, and Alice and Lajos loitered in the rear, evidently well content with each other's company.

Annette, too, increased Margaret's impatience to proceed to Zermatt by letting fall fascinating hints and suggestions in regard to her great-aunt. She threw every possible obstacle in the way of Margaret's meeting with the countess, or accepting her invitations, — hiding her gloves, disclosing stains and rents at the last moment, when quite too late to remedy defects. She was in a fever of anxiety to be off, and of apprehension of detection, and she longed for some event which would break up this, to her, very undesirable intimacy. None of her plots to hasten the departure succeeded; but the event came from an entirely unexpected quarter.

One evening, as the carriage of the countess halted at the door of the hotel, after an excursion to the Castle of Chillon, the clerk met the Judge with the well-pleased air of a man who has done his duty and deserves appreciation. "An American has inquired for you," he announced; "and I told him that you left special directions that no Americans would be received. He said he had made your acquaintance at Geneva, and you expected to meet him again. I told him that was probably the reason you were so particular in your orders to me. He flushed as red as a beet, and said, 'Oh! very well,' and went away."

"Do you remember his name?" Margaret asked.

"It was Walker," replied the clerk. "I remember that very well; for I thought it very appropriate, he walked so well and so fast. He went straight down the Mountain to Montreux, where he has doubtless lodged at the inn, and we have lost a guest; but I don't mind that, since I have done a service to Monsieur and the young ladies."

"You took me a little too seriously, my friend," said the Judge. "I had no idea that Mr. Walker was coming in this direction, and I would like very much to see him."

The three girls joined in a chorus of, "What a pity!" and, "I trust he is not greatly offended," as they mounted the stairs.

Margaret decided that an apology was due him; and the Judge wrote a kind letter, which, however, could not be sent until the morning. Livingston Walker had stepped aside, when half-way down the mountain, to allow the carriages to roll by, and, though unrecognized himself, had heard Margaret's gay laugh ring out, and had noticed that a distinguished-looking foreigner sat beside her.

Stung by the rebuff which he had just received, he decided rashly that it must have been meant for him personally by Margaret.

"She is a heartless schemer," he said to himself; "her giddy head turned by the attentions of a noble of the fifth rank. It serves me right for stopping over, on my way, to accept her grandfather's invitation. I shall know better in future."

CHAPTER V.

THE JUNGFRAU AND THE OBERLAND.

> The clouds are on the Oberland,
>   The Jungfrau snows look faint and far;
> But bright are these green fields at hand,
>   And through those fields comes down the Aar;
> And from the blue twin lakes it comes,
>   Flows by the town, the churchyard fair,
> And 'neath the garden-walk it hums,
>   The house,—and is my Marguerite there?
> MATTHEW ARNOLD.

JUDGE HOUGHTON, who was sorry for the affront which his friend had received, decided to take an early morning walk the next day, and make suitable explanations. He was, therefore, not a little disappointed to find that Livingston Walker had just left for Thun, doubtless on his way to the Jungfrau, the glacier of the Aar. A great desire to ascend the mountain in his company came over Judge Houghton. With his recent walks had come the conviction that mountaineering was not the easy matter which he had imagined, and he could not help thinking that the company of such a vigorous young climber would be of immense assistance to him. If only he could induce Margaret to deflect from her route long enough to make this ascension, they might easily overtake Mr. Walker. He returned to the hotel to find the girls discussing their plans at the breakfast-table.

Cecilia and Alice had decided that, much as they were enjoying their delightful stay at Glion, they could not remain longer. Mrs. Newton would accompany them on their Eastern journey as far as

Lucerne, and they were endeavoring to persuade Margaret to make the same decision.

Margaret, who was weary of the countess and of Glion, was quite ready to leave, but felt that she must turn her face toward Zermatt. "What do you say, grandpa?" she asked, appealing to Judge Houghton.

"I fancy the aunt will keep a few weeks longer," replied the old man eagerly. "I would like nothing better than to visit Lucerne. It is the William Tell region, and I want that for my lecture. Besides, the Jungfrau is exactly on the way. We can obtain a fine view of it from Interlaken."

The old gentleman wisely said nothing of his hope of meeting Mr. Walker, rightly thinking that for Margaret this would be no argument in favor of the plan.

Margaret consented to the wishes of the others, only stipulating that in a week's time she should proceed to Zermatt.

"Then let us go at once!" exclaimed Judge Houghton. "Off, girls, and pack your trunks, while I look up the route."

"How disappointed the countess will be!" Alice remarked. "See what lovely flowers she has sent us," and Alice pointed to a superb bouquet of Alpine roses or rhododendrons, which, however, bore the card of Lajos.

"Ah, yes! the poor countess," Margaret remarked carelessly, "and poor Lajos as well; but they cannot expect us to remain with them the rest of our natural lives."

"It seems to me that is exactly what they do expect," said Mrs. Newton; "and I feel that it is quite time that we separated."

Great was the dismay of the countess when our travellers bade her farewell. "Lucerne!" she exclaimed. "For why do you remove yourself to Lucerne? Is it not beautiful enough here?"

"It is beautiful, dear countess; but we must all go on, Alice to her mission, Cecilia to Baireuth, and I to my relatives."

"Fiddlestick!" replied the amiable lady, "zat is all as nonsense.

You must visit me at my own home; you must go back wiz me to Hungary."

It was with great difficulty that Alice persuaded her that this was impossible for the present, and it was only by promising that she would try to visit her before returning to America that the countess was induced to relinquish her hold upon her. Lajos had gone for a long tramp up the Rhone valley, and did not share in the leave-taking.

The preparations for departure were hastily made. It had been decided to drive over the Col de Jaman to Thun, and then to take the steamer across the lake to Interlaken. The carriage was at the door in an hour's time; and all took their places in high good humor, with the exception of Alice, who was a little pensive. Annette mounted to her seat beside the driver in a tremor of delight. She did not like the postponement of their visit to Zermatt, but anything was better than remaining longer under the same roof with this mysterious woman who might prove to be even the great-aunt herself.

In her trepidation she had written to her Uncle Jakob Lochwalder, asking him to inquire at The Riffel Hotel, and secure for her any information which could be obtained in reference to the Baroness Du Fais.

She would have felt even less assured if she had known that the countess had invited Margaret to visit her; and that she was even now determining that Lucerne would be a pleasant locality to visit on their return to Austria, a decision in which her nephew was certain to concur.

Judge Houghton's plot in the meantime was crowned with success, and the girls were greatly surprised as they took the steamer at Thun on the following day to meet Mr. Livingston Walker. Their surprise was mutual, and the Judge's delight unbounded. The discourtesy of the hotel clerk was explained; and all placed their camp-stools on deck, and enjoyed the lovely scenery of the lake in company. The day was perfect, good humor reigned. The young man's spirits rose, and his grievance vanished. He pointed and named out the castles on the shore as they passed them, — Chartreuse, Hunech, and that of Count de Portales. At Spiez the great mountains of the Oberland came into view; the Eiger, or giant, Mönch, or monk, and the Jungfrau, the virgin, grouped themselves in front, and the Faulhorn and Schreckhorn on the left. They had seen no such peaks as these hitherto, and exclamations of admiration were uttered on every side. Judge Houghton edged his camp-stool close to Mr. Walker's, and confided, "I dragged them all away from Glion, much against their will, simply because I was determined to ascend the Jungfrau with you."

"What, you wish the ladies to ascend the Jungfrau?"

"No, no; of course not. They are not equal to it; but it is one of the things which I came to Switzerland to do," and he pointed to the name on his alpenstock. "I must not give up the battle without a blow. The ladies will wait for us at Interlaken."

Mr. Walker was embarrassed. It was hard to tell this enthusiastic old gentleman that the climb was too difficult for him, but it was plainly his duty to dissuade him from the undertaking. He tried his best to do so, but Judge Houghton was not to be dissuaded. "I am quite as well able to do it as you," he asserted with some warmth. "And if you do not care to have me as a companion, I will go alone." It needed all of Margaret's tact to soothe his ruffled temper.

"Very well, we will see; we will see," said Mr. Walker. "The weather may be unusually favorable; and if the best guides are disengaged, it may not be impossible."

"We can never get him to the top" the young man thought with a sinking heart; "but I will not desert him."

Margaret gave him a look of gratitude, which showed that she comprehended the situation. It was a delightful thing to share a responsibility of hers, to know that he was aiding her in any way; and in such a cause he felt himself ready to carry Judge Houghton on his back to the summit of the Jungfrau. Their short sail was quickly over. The steamer stopped at Darlingen, and the passengers were conveyed from the lake of Thun by rail to Interlaken or the twin lake of Brienz.

They found Interlaken a gay watering-place, with twenty-five or more hotels, crowded with guests. Mr. Walker selected for them the Jungfraublick, on the Höheweg or main avenue, a pleasant street, shaded with walnut trees. The windows of their rooms commanded a fine view of the Jungfrau. They were comfortably lodged, but the troops of tourists who were continually coming and going had robbed Interlaken of its secluded rural air and the peasants of their unconscious simplicity.

"Beautiful as it is, I would not care to remain here long," Cecilia said; and the rest echoed the sentiment.

Margaret had fancied that she enjoyed rank, fashion, and wealth; but its continued display at Interlaken surfeited her. The orchestra, discoursing Strauss and Offenbach in the Kursaal, Swiss peasants metamorphosed into waiters in full-dress suits, flirting white napkins, and serving interminable glasses of Rhine wine, imposing equipages, with high-stepping horses, jingling chains, and gilded harnesses, a Golconda of diamonds at the breakfast-table, electric lights and telephones, and the crowd of invalids and pleasure-seekers, — all wearied her inexpressibly; and she longed to flee away to some boundless, uninhabited wilderness.

A METAMORPHOSED NATIVE OF INTERLAKEN.

If she had thought more deeply, she would have recognized the fact that she was more dissatisfied with herself than with her surroundings.

Judge Houghton on the morning after their arrival arrayed himself

THE JUNGFRAU.

in his Alpine costume, and apostrophized the Jungfrau from the balcony of his bedroom in the following terms:—

"So there you are, old lady, and in good humor, not a cloud on your brow. Just wait a moment until I have my lunch put up, and I will make your more intimate acquaintance."

Mr. Walker, who had the adjoining room, heard him speaking, and opened his blinds.

"Ah! and there you are, sleepy head!" exclaimed the Judge. "Come, let us be off, or we will not be back in time for dinner."

"I should think not," replied Mr. Walker. "Why, my dear sir, there are fifty miles of good climbing between us and the summit of the Jungfrau, for all it looks so near."

The Judge was much disappointed, and could hardly believe the statement; but he descended to the office and there made the acquaintance of a young tourist, who had similar aspirations in regard to the Jungfrau. Speedily an agreement was made between them to ascend the mountain in company; and the younger enthusiast secured the services of two of the best-known guides who happened to be looking for employment, agreeing to drive to Grindelwald, and to make the ascension from that point, on Monday of the following week.

THE JUDGE SALUTES THE JUNGFRAU.

When the Judge announced this plan at breakfast, Margaret and Mr. Walker regarded each other across the table in dismay. "But you promised to climb the mountain with Mr. Walker, grandpa!" Margaret exclaimed.

"Mr. Walker is welcome to come with me," the Judge replied.

"But you forget that he promised to take us to-day to the valley of Lauterbrunnen and the Fall of the Staubach, and you wanted to see that, too."

"So I did, so I did. I wanted to photograph it for my lecture. Is there not time for both?"

"Hardly, before Monday; but you can send word to the guides, postponing the excursion," suggested Mr. Walker.

"Hum, hum!" muttered the Judge, only half satisfied. "The guides are positively engaged for the first of next week by this Mr. Barney Jones, who cultivates athletics, and has taken the prize in several walking matches. He intends to ascend the Jungfrau, and I think it would be a good plan for us to make one party."

"I doubt the expediency of the plan," Mr. Walker replied. "There is a great difference between walking in a gymnasium on a level track and climbing mountains, and every weak link added reduces the strength of our chain."

"That may be," replied the Judge; "but this young man has been in training for a year, with Alpine mountaineering in view. He's something of a dandy, it's true; but he is acquainted with the members of the English Alpine Club, and he is provided with all the latest accoutrements. You ought to hear him talk. He knows why Whymper failed so many times on the Matterhorn, and what to do in case of avalanches. I think it would be a great help to have him with us; besides, it would make the trip cost less for us both."

At this point a servant announced that the carriage ordered to take them to Staubach had arrived, and the conversation was interrupted.

The Judge hastily pencilled a note to Mr. Jones, saying that he would not fail to be at Grindelwald on Monday.

"We have escaped one danger," Mr. Walker said to Margaret, as they found themselves together for an instant on leaving the table.

"I fear it is only postponing the evil day," she replied. "Grandpa is determined on making this ascent."

"He is no more equal to it than to travelling on foot and alone across Central Africa!" Mr. Walker exclaimed.

"I know it, and he is just as likely to take it into his head to attempt the African expedition. What can I do? I feel so utterly helpless. I had no idea of the responsibility I was assuming when I promised grandma that I would take care of him."

"Don't worry; trust it all to me. . He shall not ascend the Jungfrau; something shall occur to make him miss this opportunity."

It had been decided that Mrs. Newton and Annette should proceed with the baggage to Grindelwald and wait for the rest of the party, who would ride from Staubach over the Wenger Alp to that place.

They dined at Staubach and then struck off from the valley, following a bridle-path to the top of the Wenger Alp. It was Saturday afternoon and they had planned to pass the Sabbath at a little inn at the top in the solitude of the high Alps. It was an experience never to be forgotten, proving to be one of the most enjoyable excursions of their trip. This mountain is considered of easy ascent, and from its top wonderful views are to be obtained of the giants of the Oberland, by which it is surrounded, and especially of the Jungfrau, from which it is separated by a comparatively narrow ravine.

The trip was made on horseback (the carriage which had brought them being sent back to Interlaken) and a hostler following on foot to take back the saddle-horses to Stauback. After an hour of rather steep climbing, they paused at the village of Wengern and looked down upon the valley, which seemed from that height a narrow cleft. A rustic came from one of the houses and played upon an immense Alpine horn for their enjoyment. The blast which he blew was so mighty that the girls covered their ears and begged him to desist. The musician seemed accustomed to having his performance received in this way, and accepted the Judge's gratuity with smiling satisfaction. Their path wound now through a pine forest. The Judge, knowing that a fine view would be afforded just beyond, hurried forward, calling to the others to hasten. Cecilia and Alice urged their horses, and as Margaret and Mr. Walker had alighted and were varying the trip by walking, they were left behind with the hostler who led their horses. Mr. Walker had been talking enthusiastically of Agassiz, and Margaret listened with interest to the young man's description of his master's life in the Hotel Neuchatelois as he christened the cabin on the Aar glacier in which he and his friends lived while making their observations.

"Just what was it that Agassiz discovered in relation to glaciers?" Margaret asked. "I know that his monument in Mount Auburn is a boulder from the glacier of the Aar; but I am ashamed to say that I do not know exactly what Agassiz's discovery was. It was known before this that glaciers moved, was it not? You must not infer everything discreditable to my college from my ignorance," she added quickly, noticing the young man's momentary expression of surprise. "Remember I am only a sophomore. We take up lithological and physiographic geology next year."

"The wildest theories in regard to glaciers were held before Agassiz," Mr. Walker replied. "One scientist read a paper before the British Academy to prove that they were remnants of the deluge. It had been proved by actual observation that they moved, but the world at large had not accepted the proof. Agassiz discovered their rate of movement and many other phenomena, and drew from them very broad and overwhelming conclusions, which entirely revolutionized the theory held until that time in regard to glaciers. The scientist Hugi had built a cabin on a glacier of the Aar in 1872, and had carefully recorded its position in relation to objects near by; and when Agassiz visited the spot in 1839, he found the cabin four thousand feet lower down. For ten years he labored among the principal glaciers of the Alps, ascertaining their rate of motion by determining by triangulation the exact position of the more prominent rocks, and returning year after year to mark the change. He made careful meteorological observations upon the internal temperature of the glaciers by boring to a great depth through the ice and nserting registering thermometers. He caused himself to be lowered into crevasses, and ascended many peaks regarded as inaccessible, and his companions under his direction studied the flora and fauna of the region, and the mysterious red snow—"

"Pray, what is that?" Margaret asked.

"It was discovered under the microscope to consist of myriads of infusoria, a low order of plant life. It is not infrequently met with in this region."

Shortly after this they emerged from the wood and arrived at the hotel where a magnificent view opened before them of the Jungfrau, just across the ravine of the Trumleten. It seemed only at the distance of a rifle shot and all its inmost recesses were opened up to them, but from this point it was utterly inaccessible. The Judge stood among a party gazing spell-bound at its steep incline wrapped in a long, unbroken, winding sheet of snow. As he looked a long rift or crack was distinctly seen across one of them, succeeded a moment later by a loud report, and an immense cake or snow-field slipped away from the side of the mountain, coasted down the precipice, bursting into a flurry of fine white powder and disappearing in the precipice at their feet.

"POSITIVELY FWITEFUL."

"An avalanche!" every one exclaimed in a breath, and a young exquisite in patent leathers and a silk hat turned and murmured— "It is fwiteful! It is positively fwiteful. Think of being cwushed flatter than an opewa hat by one of those beastly avalanches! How fwitefully disagweeable."

It was Mr. Barney Jones who had come over armed with all the approved methods of the Alpine Club, and who then and there relinquished his ambition of climbing "that blawsted Jungfwaw. Because it isn't blawsted, you know," he explained. "No joke, 'pon honor, if they would only blawst away the snow, and constwuct a gwaded pawth, then there would be some weason in the undertaking."

Other avalanches followed. They were not so frightful to look at, as to hear; for it was necessary to remind oneself that what seemed only a flurry of white powder near at hand was miles away, and covered a vast extent, while the detonations were tremendous and, conveyed through the marvellously pure air with perfect distinctness, seemed like the reverberations of thunder. An American is said to have once remarked of the same scene, "I tell you, when I heard the first avalanche fall, I thought the whole creation was tumbling to pieces. And yet 'twas no more to look at than a barrel of flour tipped over!"

The cone of the Jungfrau is so pointed that only one person can stand on it at once and the last part of the ascension is usually effected with ladders.

The Judge, seeing that his hero had given up the ascent, also reluctantly acknowledged it impossible. After supper they all watched the sunset flushing the peaks, and dying away into cool gray, then the mists rose from the valleys and shrouded the mountains, and a cold wind from the Jungfrau seemed to freeze the marrow in their bones. The moon was coming up and touching the crests and turning them to mighty silver candlesticks, but the cold grew more and more intense and they were glad to take refuge by the blazing fire of the inn. The landlord's daughter played on the zithern, but the room was filled with tourists, and when thoroughly warmed the girls retired to their simple bedroom. They lay awake for some time listening to the notes of the zithern rising from the room below and softened by distance, and watching the white moonlight streaming in from the large window until moonlight and music melted into their dreams.

The next morning nearly all of the tourists went on their journey. The landlord told them of some open-air preaching within walking distance, and the rest set out for the convocation. The preacher was very simple and unimpassioned in his address, but the peasants listened devoutly with bared heads, and the singing, with the great mountains all about them, was very impressive.

"This is the grandest cathedral I ever saw," said Cecilia.

"I was reading to grandpa only the other night what Ruskin says of the mountains," Margaret said, as they walked back to the little hotel. "I copied a part in my journal," and Margaret read:—

"'They seem to have been built for the human race as at once their schools and cathedrals; full of treasures of illuminated manuscript for the scholar, kindly in simple lessons to the worker, quiet in pale cloisters for the thinker, glorious in holiness for the worshipper. Great cathedrals of the earth, with their gates of rock, pavements of cloud, choirs of stream and stone, altars of snow, and vaults of purple traversed by the continual stars.'"

They spent the afternoon in a secluded nook, reading quietly part of the time, or talking in subdued tones, but listening more frequently and watching for the avalanches which, loosened by the mid-day sun, plunged at intervals into the gorge. They had lost the sense of fright which the first impression of the mountain and the precipice had made upon them, but the feeling of awe deepened. All the life of Interlaken and its like seemed petty and contemptible; great thoughts and aspirations filled Margaret's soul; it seemed to her that she had never been so near God before.

The next morning they descended to Grindelwald, walking all the way, and accomplishing it before dinner. No one was wearied but Judge Houghton, who was kindly assisted by Mr. Walker. The grand peak of the Wetterhorn rose in front of them, and the Faulhorn loomed on their left toward the north, while on the right was the lower glacier of Grindelwald. It was their first view of a real glacier —a great frozen river composed by the alternate melting and freezing of the snowfall on the different peaks, and the snows of each season

THE WELLHORN AND WETTERHORN.

pressing downward and onward the deposit of the last. The Finsteraarhorn is the centre of the glacial system of the Oberland, from its sides and between it and the surrounding mountains sweep the great glacier of the Aar and its smaller branches. The Finsteraarhorn has rightly been called the "monarch of mountains." It overtops all its surrounding brothers, rising to the height of fourteen thousand one hundred and six feet. One author says of it, "It rises up like a huge tower from the Hetsch glacier, Viescher glaciers, Grindelwald and Finsteraar glaciers, and looking as if in rising it had dragged part of them up with it; for there are pillars and buttresses of ice reaching to its topmost summit, and connecting it with its neighbors on the east and west, the fair Jungfrau, the round-headed Monk, the sharp-pointed Eiger and gloomy Shreckhorn, the Wetterhorns (and others), which stand on either side of the monarch and form his court."

As they passed the Grindelwald glacier Mr. Walker gave them much interesting information in regard to it and other glaciers. He explained the origin of the curious mushroom-shaped tables and the small wells; the former caused by the larger stones shading the ice beneath them and keeping it from melting, so that while the surface around was lowered by the action of the sun the rock was hoisted in air by an ever-growing pedestal. The small stones, on the contrary, are heated through by the sun and cause the ice to melt more rapidly, forming the narrow wells.

The Judge remarked on the size of the stones in the moraine at the foot of the glacier. He had not supposed that the debris would be so considerable or so difficult to cross.

"Then you have not heard the definition of a moraine given by a member of the Alpine Club?" Mr. Walker asked; "the young man described it as one hundred thousand cartloads of stones carefully piled up by Nature on scientific principles with a view to the dislocation of the human ankle."

Grindelwald was wilder and more simple than Interlaken. There were fewer tourists and the peasants more unsophisticated, though the girls were still importuned to purchase wood-carvings and lace, and small boys followed them with specimens from the glacier, crystals and pebbles, and bouquets of Alpine flowers. At this point they rejoined Mrs. Newton and Annette, who had not cared to take the mountain excursion, and here in front of the hotel they found Mr. Barney Jones in hot altercation with one of the guides who had been engaged to ascend the Jungfrau. The young athlete was as eager now to give up the excursion as he had been to undertake it; but the guides held him to his bargain, and the hotel-keeper took sides with them. The Judge offered to pay the sum which he had previously agreed upon to settle the matter; and Mr. Walker stepped in as mediator.

MR. BARNEY JONES IN DIFFICULTIES.

"It isn't the money," said the recusant Alpinist, "but the howid cweatures seem to regard me as their lawful pwey and are determined to lug me along body and bones. I'll pay the fellahs whatever I've pwomised if they'll only let me off from making the twip."

This being explained to the guides, everything was amicably arranged, and from Grindelwald our friends proceeded on the next day to Meiringen. Here Mr. Walker took leave of them, turning off toward the right on his way to the hospice of the Grimsel and thence to the glacier of the Aar. Annette suggested that this was the most direct route to Zermatt, and all regretted the ending of their pleasant intercourse, and none more than Mr. Walker himself. Judge Houghton would gladly have accompanied him, but the young man assured Margaret that the mountaineering which he must now undertake was much too difficult for the Judge. "The Rigi is quite enough for him," he said to her; "and I think that when he has once made that ascent he will be satisfied. I would like very much to take him with me across some of the passes. After I have finished my Agassiz pilgrimage, I would like to make such a trip as your friend thought of, and follow up Napoleon as an engineer. I will be through with my glacier work in about a month from the present time. Have I your permission to join you then?"

"Grandpa will be delighted to go with you, I am sure," Margaret replied. "We shall be at Zermatt in all probability."

"That is a dangerous point for any one afflicted with the *mania scandens*. If your grandfather manifests any wild desire to scale the Matterhorn, write me at the Grimsel, and I will fly to him at once."

Margaret laughed, but underneath the apparent lightness on either side, she was certain that here was a friend who could be depended upon in any real need; and he knew that he was ready to do all that he had said, and more than he dared to offer, for her sake.

CHAPTER VI.

LUCERNE.

> Yonder lies
> The lake of the Four Forest Towns, apparelled
> In light, and lingering like a village maiden.
> . . . . . . Overhead,
> Shaking his cloudy tresses loose in air,
> Rises Pilatus with his windy pines.
>
> LONGFELLOW.

WHEN the party took the diligence at Meiringen, which was to carry them over the Brunig towards Lucerne, even the weather seemed to sympathize with the low state of feeling caused by the parting. All the skies in the Oberland had been fair; all their days bright and pleasant; but now a heavy fog wrapped the mountains. As they alighted and looked back, just before reaching the post-house on the summit of the Col de Brunig, hoping to obtain the traditional farewell view of all the mountains whose names end in *horn*, a dense gray curtain was stretched between them and the "Delectable Mountains," and Margaret felt that all the beautiful past was blotted out.

At Alpnach Mr. Walker had told them to look for the chute, down which logs are slid from the pine forests on the slopes of Mount Pilatus to the lake, a distance of eight miles. The slide is paved with over twenty-five thousand trees, stripped of their bark, and laid at an angle of ten to eighteen degrees. Logs shoot down the eight miles in less than six minutes.

It was not actually raining when they reached Alpnach, on the shore of Lake Lucerne, but Annette pointed to Mount Pilatus towering above them, and repeated the old German proverb: —

> "*Hat Pilatus sein hut
> Dann wird das Wetter gut,
> Trägt er aber einen Degen
> So giebts wohl sicher regen.*"

Which has been translated:—

> If Pilatus wears his hood,
> Then the weather's always good;
> If he draws his dirk again,
> We shall surely then have rain.

They looked, and saw that, instead of the round cloud which usually caps the mountain's head, a ragged, cloudy streamer, shaped something like a waving sword, was flying like a storm-signal toward Lucerne. A storm of wind, the avant-courier of the tempest gathering in the Oberland, was evidently raging at the top of the mountain, though unfelt in the lower air.

"What an excellent place that would be for Old Probability's office," the Judge remarked.

"But not an enviable station for the signal officer," Margaret replied.

PILATUS, LAKE OF LUCERNE.

"There is an interesting legend connected with the mountain," said Cecilia; "have you never heard it?" When the bustle occasioned by their transfer from the diligence to the little steamer which was to convey them to Lucerne had subsided, she told them the legend somewhat as follows: —

"After the death of the Saviour, Pilate so greatly mismanaged the government of Judea that he was recalled by Tiberius to Rome, and an examination made into his affairs. Most mysteriously the emperor cleared him, and re-instated him in favor. Other charges were made against him, with like result, when it was suggested that Pilate used magical arts to maintain his influence over the emperor. He was examined by his enemies, and it was discovered that he wore the Saviour's robe as an amulet underneath his toga, and when this was stripped off, the emperor immediately threw him into prison. Here Pilate committed suicide, and his body was cast into the Tiber. Storms and tempests visited Rome, and the indignant river cast the corpse upon the shore. It was then carried into Gaul and thrown into the Rhine; but the heathen river also refused to cover the criminal, and after many vicissitudes the body was finally sunk in a little lake on the top of the mountain which now bears the Roman governor's name. Even here he refused to rest, until exorcised by a travelling student from Salamanca, learned in the Black Art, who laid him under a spell, forcing him to consent to but one holiday during the year, and that on Good Friday. On this night a terrible figure, dressed in the red robes of magistracy, is sometimes seen by the peasants, but whoever beholds him dies within the following year."

"What nonsense," commented the Judge; "does the superstition still exist?"

"Hardly now, but it died a lingering death. It was said that Pilate's anger was excited whenever the water of his lake was disturbed. At one time all persons were forbidden to visit the lake, and a guardian was posted on the mountain side to keep them at a distance. In 1337 six priests were imprisoned for ascending the mountain. In 1518 four enlightened men obtained permission to investigate the myth. They ascended the mountain, hurled stones

HOTEL NATIONAL, LUCERNE.

into the lake and dared Pilate to do his worst. Oddly enough a severe storm followed, and the superstition was confirmed."

Almost as Cecilia finished speaking, the storm which had been gathering about the head of the haunted mountain burst upon them, first in violent gusts of wind which nearly tore their hats from their heads, and then in a steady down-pour of rain. By this time, however, the boat had nearly reached Lucerne, and they were soon housed in the Hotel National which fronts the quay.

Their baggage had arrived before them, having been sent on from Interlaken, and the girls were soon engaged in dressing for dinner — a custom which had not been kept up in the Oberland.

Margaret gave a little sigh as she shook out the ruffles of her embroidered Swiss gown, and heated her hair-crimper in the gas. "I feel as if I had been lifted out of myself, and had been allowed to fall to earth once more. I don't believe it will be so easy to be good here as it was among the mountains. I foresee that now we shall have Glion over again."

Her foresight seemed to have something prophetic about it; for as they entered the dining-room, a tall man in heavily frogged and decorated military dress rose from a table at the extreme end of the room and came forward to meet them, while a little old woman in black, who occupied the next seat, flourished her napkin and beckoned wildly with a tall fan.

Alice exclaimed, "Lajos!" and Margaret, "The Countess!" but in very different tones.

The Countess was evidently overjoyed. She kissed the girls all around, not even forgetting Alice, but she saluted Margaret on both cheeks and held her off and gazed at her with rapture. "How well you are looking! And you have on ze dress I gave you. It becomes to you very well. Where have you been all zis time? It is an eternity I have wait for you."

"It is only four or five days, countess, and we have had a positively heavenly time."

"The scenery was magnificent," Alice was saying to Lajos, "but really it was a little lonely."

"I am glad of that," replied Lajos. "Aunt and I have been devoured with loneliness."

"But Glion was not a desolate wilderness, and Lucerne does not seem to be deserted."

"True, the hotel is crowded, but what objectionable people!"

"There is one comfort," Margaret remarked as she surveyed the *table d'hote*, "Calumet and Hecla are not here."

"I have found some one very similar," Lajos replied. "An American who monopolizes the newspapers in the reading-room, actually sitting on those which he is not reading, but making up for it by obligingly giving quotations from the stock market, and shouting at intervals: 'Bell Telephone, firm and steady!' 'Pullman Car, active!' 'Atchison depressed!' 'Copper falling!' or other ejaculations as remarkable."

STOCK QUOTATIONS.

The countess had purchased tickets for them for a concert to take place that evening. "How did you know that we would arrive to-night?" Margaret asked.

"She has bought them regularly every evening," Lajos explained; "and you see she has kept these seats for you at this table, assuring the head waiter every day that you would certainly be here for the next meal."

"Zat is nossing, zat is nossing, and who is it who read effery time ze arrival at all ze hotel? And who promenade himself ze town around to meet zese young ladies?"

"I will not pretend that I did not have some personal interest in the matter; but then, my dear aunt, I could not see you so impatient without doing all I could to relieve your anxiety."

"Fiddlestick, zat is not polite; more, zat is not true, and now who will go to ze concert?"

Mrs. Newton, the Judge, and Cecilia were weary, and begged to be excused, and a *partie quarré* was formed of the countess and Margaret, Alice and Lajos. "Quite as in the old days," Margaret thought, hardly realizing that the old days were only last week. But there was this difference now,—the countess placed her arm inside that of Alice, and peremptorily beckoned Lajos to offer his to Margaret; and yet Margaret did not seem to have declined at all in her favor.

Margaret felt herself exhilarated as they drove through the wet streets, the lamps reflected in the glistening pavements, and still more so as they took their places in the brilliantly lighted hall filled with beautiful women in full dress, the odor of hot-house flowers, and the entrancing strains of a fine orchestra.

Their seats were not quite together, but were separated by an aisle, so that Margaret found herself for the first time alone with Lajos, in a crowd to be sure, but virtually alone, and she was obliged to confess that he was not entertaining. Perhaps the reason was that he was so fond of music, but he scarcely spoke to her. Once he roused himself and asked if they had met the engineer again of whom Alice had spoken. "Oh, yes!" Margaret replied, "and he was greatly interested in your plan of making a Napoleon pilgrimage. I really wish you could meet and arrange to make it together. He will soon furnish his observations on the Aar glacier. His address is the hospice of the Grimsel; if you cared to write him he would come to Lucerne."

"I? Oh, no!" Lajos replied hastily; "I don't want him in Lucerne; quite the contrary. Do you think he admires Miss Alice?"

"Why, of course; every one does." And Lajos relapsed into silence.

Their intercourse during the week that followed was carried on after the same plan. Alice was now the countess's chosen companion, and Margaret and Lajos, without any wish of their own, were constantly thrown together. Just what the countess had in view by this arrangement no one quite understood. Mrs. Newton, at all events, was well satisfied. Her quick instincts had boded no good from the evident pleasure which Lajos and Alice took in each other's society so long as the countess maintained her prejudice.

Margaret was selfishly glad to be relieved from attendance on the countess; Lajos possibly hoped that Alice would win the heart of his patroness, and too polite to allow his indifference to Margaret to render him rude, calmly accepted the role assigned him. Alice showed by no word or sign that the countess's society was not in all respects as agreeable as that of her nephew, and was as sweet and unruffled, as thoughtful and unselfish, as ever.

Annette's displeasure on finding that intercourse was again established with the Countess Krajova can better be imagined than described. She was quite sure now that this was not her former mistress. There were points of dissimilarity which struck her more forcibly as she studied the strange woman. Moreover, a letter had arrived from her uncle at Zermatt, informing her that the landlord of the Riffel Hotel was positive that the Baroness Du Fais had died the year following Annette's emigration to America. This was reassuring; but if this mysterious countess was not Margaret's aunt, who was she? And how had she come into possession of the vinaigrette with the well-known crest?

Annette had surreptitiously entered the countess's rooms during her absence, and had looked over all her belongings. There was nothing marked with the fire-brand crest with the exception of the vinaigrette, and no scrap of writing to identify her with the Baroness. In her eagerness to suppress any link of evidence, Annette committed the mistake of stealing the vinaigrette. The theft was not immediately traced to her, but the countess missed the keepsake which was evidently one with associations, and talked of it continually, describing the crest minutely. Annette recognized her blunder, and trembled for fear of detection. Something must be done at once, and she accordingly accosted Margaret one evening with the information that no amount of reward would induce her to remain another day in Lucerne.

"It is evident," Annette said very pertly, "that you do not care to find your relatives; but as for me, I am not going to neglect mine any longer, and, with your permission, I will leave you and take the direct route to Zermatt by way of the Visp valley."

"You must not speak to me in that way, Annette. I have not lost my interest in my unknown relatives; but I prefer to be the mistress of my own movements, and to remain in Lucerne until after the great festival. It would be very foolish to leave the city before it takes place when it is so near at hand. Meantime, you are perfectly at liberty to go on in advance of us, and to announce our coming to my aunt."

This plan was accordingly decided upon, and Annette left at once.

The time was approaching for the annual festival in honor of William Tell, and great preparations were in progress for its celebra-

ANNETTE TAKES HER DEPARTURE.

tion upon the lake. Many anxious eyes were turned toward the heavens, for the rain still descended, and Pilatus pointed a threatening dagger toward Lucerne.

But Cecilia's music drove away *ennui*, or they read in turn aloud, while the countess worked upon an interminable piece of embroidery. Occasionally the clouds lifted, and they slipped out to see the sights of the city. The monument to the Swiss Guards who fell on the 10th of August, 1792, while defending Louis XVI of France and his family from the attacks of the revolutionists, is a very noble one. It is from a design by Thorwaldsen, and is cut from the natural rock. It represents a dying lion protecting a shield which bears the device of the Bourbon lilies. Over the cave in which the lion rests, are carved the words, "*Helvetiorum fidei ac virtuti*," — "To the valor and fidelity of the Swiss," — and beneath are the names of the fallen heroes.

The countess repeated some lines written by a Frenchman who admired their heroism more than the cause for which it was shown: —

> "Fidèles au serment que l'erreur a dicté
> Généreux défenseurs d'une injuste querelle,
> Vous, morts en combattant contre la liberté,
> Vous méritez bien mieux d'avoir vécu pour elle."

The countess always called Margaret into her room after these excursions, and asked her what she had seen, and very often the intelligent old lady supplemented the sight-seeing with some interesting or valuable bit of information.

On one occasion Margaret ridiculed an old stove which she had seen among the trophies of the city museum. "I presume it was the one on which Winkelried's mother baked his brown bread," she remarked derisively.

"My tear, how is it possible you can not haf heard ze history to zat stove?" the countess asked. "Zat is one very old legend. Ze stove have formerly stand in ze guild-room of ze butchers. It was in sirteen sirty-two, when zare was plot to deliver Lucerne to ze Austriano. One small boy hear ze plot, but ze conspirators catch him and make him to swear he will tell no living human being what he justly did hear. For well zey know zat ze Swiss boy's conscience not suffer him to tell a lie. But look you, zat Swiss boy not altogether one fool. He run into ze guild-room, at zat time full of butcher, and he cry out to ze stove, 'O stove, I have promise to tell no human being, but I declare unto zee zis plot.' Zen he tell it all, and of course ze butchers know it too, and ze plot is spoil and ze city safed."

"Swiss boys do not seem to be lacking in ready wit," remarked Mrs. Newton. "I remember to have read of one, a boy of St. Gall, who brought milk each morning to the castle of a nobleman. On one occasion the nobleman asked him some questions which he answered saucily, whereupon he was told that the next time he appeared near the castle the dog should be set upon him. The boy came the next morning, carrying his milk-cans as usual, when the nobleman, out of pure wantonness, set a fierce bull-dog upon the boy, who coolly lifted the cover of one of his cans; a huge cat sprung from it and flew at the dog, whose attention was fully engrossed by its unexpected antagonist, while the boy walked slowly away laughing derisively."

The river Reuss issues from the lake at Lucerne, and is here very swift and strong. It is crossed by two long and curious bridges. One of them, the Kappelbrücke, is covered, and the interior is hung with seventy strange old pictures celebrating the acts of St. Maurice. Although, as we have explained, Lajos was generally Margaret's escort, it happened that he accompanied Mrs. Newton and Alice on their visit to this bridge. It was a dark day, and they soon tired of peering into the shadows and trying to make out the subjects of the paintings, and they turned to watch the shipping.

"The Swiss seem particularly fond of representations of death," Alice said.

"They have death before them more familiarly than the inhabitants of the plain," Lajos replied; "perhaps that is the reason that they do not seem to fear it, and are ready, when occasion calls, to become heroes like Arnold Von Winkelried, who

> "For victory shaped an open space,
> By gathering with a wide embrace
> Into his single heart, a sheaf
> Of fatal Austrian spears."

BRIDGE OF LUCERNE.

"There is one thing which I do not quite understand," said Alice. "You are an Austrian, and yet you are constantly admiring the enemies of Austria — Napoleon, Arnold Von Winkelried, Venice, all have your sympathy. It is just so with the countess. She is always praising liberty, — America's struggle for independence, the war in Bulgaria against the Turks, and the French Revolution; and yet it seems to me that Austria is one of the most despotic of despotisms."

"She is; Russia is a republic in comparison. To understand our position, I must remind you that my aunt and I are only Austrians in so far that our country belongs to Austria. We are Hungarians, and my aunt's family were all patriots. Although they belonged to the aristocratic class, they held advanced ideas in regard to liberty. My aunt's brothers were students at the University of Vienna, at the time of the French Revolution. They were in the deputation of two thousand professors and students who presented a petition to the emperor, asking for the following measures of reform: religious liberty, freedom of the press, and a national legislature in which the people should be represented."

"Of course this wild demand was refused?"

"No; the emperor was frightened, and while secretly negotiating with foreign powers for aid, he temporized by granting their request. The advocates of reform in Hungary felt that this was the time to strike for their rights, and Kossuth, with a hundred and fifty Hungarian gentlemen, visited Vienna and made the same demand which had been presented by the students. Kossuth was the idol of the hour, and the emperor, feeling himself powerless before this mighty popular wave of feeling, granted the demand of Hungary. A wonderful bloodless revolution was effected. Hungary adopted a constitution emancipating its serfs and giving prince and peasant equal political rights."

"That was an occasion where it happened well for the country that its chief ruler was a coward."

"If the event had not proved that his word was as little to be trusted as his courage. All of his promises were unscrupulously broken, and the Austrian army sent against the Hungarians as rebels. It was a war of devastation, towns and villages were burned, and the greatest cruelties inflicted; but the Hungarians resisted bravely and routed the Austrians again and again. The populace of Vienna were in sympathy with them, and rose in revolution. The emperor fled, but returning, reinforced by his army, took the city by storm, and subjected it to still more rigorous despotism. Still the war raged all over Hungary, and the emperor, seeing that he could not hope to crush his subjects, besought foreign aid. Russia responded by sending an army of a hundred and sixty thousand men to the aid of Austria, and though the struggle was maintained for some time longer, it was evident that there was no longer any hope. The Hungarian army surrendered, but Kossuth and many other Hungarians, among whom were my aunt's father and brothers, fled the country, escaping first to Turkey, and from thence to England and to America. Since that time my aunt has never seen these relatives, and now you can understand why we love liberty."

"I see," Alice replied; "but since then Hungary has gained what she asked, has she not?"

"In great measure. It came in 1865, after Austria's humiliation in being set aside from the old Germanic confederation when Prussia became the leading power. Austria no longer held her old prestige, and it was necessary for her to listen to the demands of her children, and Hungary received her birthright. My aunt, who had gone into exile with her mother when her relatives had fled the country with Kossuth, and had lived much of the time in retirement in Switzerland, returned to Hungary, when it became evident that a new order of things was to be ushered in, and the constitutional rights of the states would be respected by Austria. She was a young girl when she fled; a woman not in her first youth, but at the height of her beauty and of her intellectual powers when she returned. She entered society, and my uncle, who belonged to an old Austrian family, saw her in Vienna, was charmed by her many excellent qualities, and married her. I wish you could have known her then as I still remember her — a brilliant and fascinating woman. She has had much trouble, and age and disappointment have made her what you now see."

"I should think that her trouble ended at the time of which you speak. Freedom secured for her country, a happy marriage, rank, wealth, — what more could she need to make her happy?"

"Her father and mother died shortly after this, and her brothers, from whom she had heard occasionally up to this time, never returned. Her youth had fled; there was no longer the old power to hold out against continued disappointment. Waiting and longing wrought its work upon her, and she grew suddenly old when the conviction was borne in upon her that they would never return. Then her husband died, and now I am the nearest that she has left, who am only her husband's nephew. She is as kind and loving as an own mother, and when I am tempted to think her exacting I remember all that she has suffered, and I look upon her with admiration."

Alice was silent; it did not seem to her that even with this cross light upon her history the countess was particularly worthy of admiration; but she knew Lajos the better for their conversation. The confidence already established between them was strengthened, and his complaisance to all the pettish demands of the countess no longer seemed to be dancing attendance on a legacy. Without apologizing for her foibles he evidently wished to beg Alice's consideration for his aunt. It was as though he had said, "I want you to like her, and I think that if you understood her history you would be lenient to her faults."

If this conversation had been carried on with Margaret, the mention of exiled brothers would have suggested her grandfather, but Alice had never heard the strange story.

"Look!" exclaimed Mrs. Newton, "the clouds are breaking away. This looks like a final clearing up. We shall have fine weather after all for the Tell festival."

CHAPTER VII.

THE TELL FESTIVAL.

> The ranges stood
> Transfigured in the silver flood.
> Their snows were flashing cold and keen,
> Dead white, save where some sharp ravine
> Took shadow, or the sombre green
> Of hemlocks turned to pitchy black,
> Against the whiteness at their back!

WHILE the conversation just reported was in progress the Judge had been enjoying a tête-a-tête with the countess.

"How we old people live our lives some more in ze tear children," she had said. "My heart it wrap up in Lajos, and to see him what you call settle in life. My husband's will shall leave to him one nice castle, and zere is always his pay as officer in ze army. He is an eligible *parti*, and I do assure you I am very difficult about him. I have ze proposals most advantageous from some of ze best families in Europe, but no I have one little hope that will not quite extinguish itself that he will marry ze child of a friend to me for whom I have him reserve. My husband have share this hope, for ze young lady have property of which my husband was what you call guardian. My friend have put in my husband's care, and he have put it wiz some mines of his own, and now zat mines have swallow zose money, and it cannot come out, which is my husband's or his ward's. But my friend say zat make no difference if so Lajos marry ze young lady. And so my friend and my husband make zeir wills. Zey shall have ze mines together if zey marry themselves. If ze young lady refuse to marry herself wiz Lajos, zen he shall have zat mines, and if Lajos will not marry zose young lady, zen he shall not take zat mines no more. It is a great mix up, and it shall all be decide when zose young lady shall come of age."

The Judge listened with scant interest; he could hardly be said to listen at all so far. He thought the lady very voluble and a trifle absurd, and when she asked him of the fortunes of the three young ladies under his care, it seemed to him that she was simply inquisitive; but he told her frankly that both Cecilia and Alice were portionless, though independent maidens; Cecilia making a good support for herself by teaching music, and Alice a devoted missionary.

"Then Miss Newton is a religieuse and will never marry. She has what we call a vocation. It is sad, and she so young and pretty. And Miss Boylston's position is not to be sought of; but your grandchild, Miss Houghton?"

It chanced that Margaret's family name had not been mentioned, and the countess had taken it for granted that it was the same as that of the Judge.

"Oh, Margaret will have a snug little fortune when I die!" the old gentleman replied.

"And you have brought her to Europe to marry her?"

"Marry my granddaughter! Why, I couldn't do that, even if my wife were not living!"

"Monsieur does not understand me. You have brought her to Europe to find for her a husband?"

"Well, no; not exactly. Margaret brought me to Europe; and there is no need of our bothering our heads about finding her a husband. No danger but plenty of admirable young Americans will find her; and if there is anything that our girls are particular about, it is to have their own choice."

"So?" said the countess. She was far from understanding the Judge, and she was surprised that he did not appreciate the great desirability of her nephew as a possible husband for Margaret. The Judge's apathy only raised Margaret's value in her eyes. It was nothing to her that Lajos thought Margaret frivolous and mercenary. Could he have heard her reckless chatter that night, as she discussed him with her friends, he would have felt himself justified in this conclusion. And yet he did not know Margaret, nor Margaret herself; for it was her worse nature, her worldly, ambitious self, that was uppermost that evening.

"Girls," she said, "haven't we had a beautiful time to-day?"

"Yes, indeed," Alice replied; "I think I never in one day saw so lovely a sunset."

Margaret laughed softly. "I didn't refer to the beauties of nature, dear, but to the beauties of human nature recently displayed."

"You mean by the countess; she is certainly very eccentric."

"She is a precious old termagant! What a life she leads her dear nephew Lajos, and every one connected with her! She seems to have taken a fancy to me. Just wouldn't I be a discipline and a revelation to her, if I were in Lajos' place. I wonder whether my unknown relative is anything like her? Think of finding a madame the countess, with servants in livery, and a coat of arms on the carriage door, and a castle in the Carpathians. It makes me wild with envy."

"Even when handicapped by such an aunt?" Cecilia asked.

"Why not? I am tremendously fond of the good things of this world, and I would be willing to give a good deal for the right to be —"

"Miserable," suggested Alice, as an appropriate ending. "I cannot conceive of a more unhappy position than to be dependent upon a benefactress whom you do not love."

At this point Judge Houghton knocked at the door of the little sitting-room. "It is time you girls were in bed," he said — but he paused at the door, admiring the pretty picture.

"Did you have a pleasant chat with the countess, grandpa?"

"She is, without exception, the most singular female I ever met," the Judge replied. "She asked me the most personal questions in regard to each of you. I began to think that she was passing you in review as possible wives for her nephew, but she disabused my mind of that idea by assuring me that she was saving him up for a distant relation. One of his Austrian cousins, I presume, and I can only explain her questions by attributing them to pure abnormal curiosity. I thought I would just mention that the young man is contracted, that there might be no heart-burning or scheming in relation to him." The Judge said this with a sly twinkle; for he well knew the indignation which his remark would create.

MARGARET AND ALICE DISCUSS LAJOS.

Margaret laughed scornfully. "The very idea — that iceberg! And yet he is quite a respectable iceberg," she added, after her grandfather had left the room. "Do you know I am more than ever inclined to regret that the countess is not my aunt, or I the distant relative for whom the magnificent Lajos is so tenderly guarded."

Alice looked up quickly. "Do you really care for him, Margaret?" and again Margaret laughed her scorn.

"And would you marry a man whom you do not love?"

"Why not, if there were no pretence?"

"And if he did not love you?"

"Then I think it would be perfectly fair. I am sure that the

Count Lajos and I would make a perfectly matched couple," she continued, only half in banter. "He does not look as if he was capable of warm affection, and as I am sure that I am not, I repeat that we seem to have been created for one another."

A rich glow burned on Alice's cheek. "I do not think you understand him," she said. "I am sure that he is capable of very true affection, but I do not believe he is happy in this engagement."

"Then why doesn't he break it?"

"Probably his aunt's favor and fortune are at stake."

"Then if he cares more for the fortune than for his freedom, I do not see that he deserves our pity."

"Nor I; and as I can't quite believe that he is so base as that, I am sure there must be some other reason."

"I do not think so; he is simply under his aunt's thumb. She can make him do exactly as she likes. He would marry me if she wished him to do so." And the thought flashed through Margaret's mind, "I have only to be nice to the countess and she would throw over this anciently-agreed-upon marriage and insist upon Lajos marrying me."

The day dawned for the Tell festival, clear and perfect, greatly to the delight of thousands of expectant people. Steamers and barges set out in the morning from Lucerne, making the circuit of the lake, and stopping on the way to Fluelen at all the villages to collect the peasants in their holiday attire.

Lajos had engaged a steam yacht for the party, and they followed in the wake of a great steamer, on which a band was playing merrily and from which flags and streamers were fluttering. The great banner of the Swiss Confederacy overtopped all, while the escutcheons of the four forest cantons, which include the Lake of Lucerne, were displayed on broad shields on the sides of the boat. The crowd on deck, in their gayly-colored costumes, gave the steamer a very brilliant appearance. In honor of the day, two of the three girls had

THE RIGI, FROM LUCERNE.

dressed in the costume of the Canton of Uri, which consists of red petticoats and stockings, black velvet bodice, and full white waist, with square velvet collars embroidered in silver. Silver chains were fastened to each corner of the collar, hanging loosely under the arms. These, with other silver ornaments, were furnished by the countess. Margaret wore the still more lavish ornaments of a peasant of Unterwalden. One adjunct of the costume they did not adopt, — the maple-wood sandals which slip with every step, and make a noisy clapping on the stone pavements. Without these it was impossible to realize their wish to pass as peasant girls among the peasants. There were discrepancies, too, in their head gear. And as they stood together later, before the porch of the church at Altdorf (see Frontispiece), they made a pretty picture for the Judge to photograph; but every true peasant knew that they were masquerading.

A SWISS MAIDEN.

They stopped at the Grütli, which tradition says was the trysting-place of the three patriots of Schwyz who founded the Swiss Confederacy; and then glided on past the Mythenstein, a rock rising from the waters of the lake, on which a grateful people have chiselled an inscription in honor of Schiller, who made the name of their hero, William Tell, famous in literature.

The boat paused for a few moments at the Tellenplatte, where stands the famous chapel to Tell, on the spot where he is supposed to have sprung on shore and escaped; but the shrine of the pilgrimage was the church at Altdorf. All the boats came to anchor at Fluelen; a procession was formed, which proceeded on foot to Altdorf, while those who did not care to take part in the procession bestowed themselves in the carriages, omnibuses, and vehicles of every description which were in waiting. All the village of Altdorf came out to meet them, singing patriotic songs and bearing garlands. Mottoes were displayed on the fronts of the houses. Wreaths and garlands of evergreen and of flowers were interspersed with bunting and fluttering ribbons. The Schutz Verein, in a sort of Robin Hood costume, carrying cross-bows, came from the gymnasium. The Capuchins, in their long brown gowns with knotted rope girdles, marched from their monastery, chanting and carrying processional crosses and candles; and the nuns marshalled the children. A bishop in white, holding his hand aloft in blessing, and priests in scarlet or in black robes, swinging censers and sprinkling holy water, stood upon the church steps. As the processions approached, the bishop turned and led the way into the church, where mass was said.

TELL'S CHAPEL, LAKE OF LUCERNE.

At Altdorf all the associations connected with William Tell concentrate. It was here that Gesler's hat was supposed to have been raised upon the pole, here Tell shot the apple from his son's head, and here Tell was born. All this according to the legend which Schiller has immortalized and which is now called in question by doubting antiquarians. It is in vain that historians now declare that the hero of Switzerland is a myth; the peasants have believed in him too firmly and for too many generations. It would be as easy to convince the American that George Washington never existed.

The girls turned from the main part of the church to the sacristy, where the costly gifts shown them testified to the faith of the princes as well as peasants, and having viewed these, all strolled through the town and a little way up the hill to secure the fine view. Again, by some magic attraction, Alice and Lajos walked together; Margaret and Cecilia following, and Mrs. Newton, the countess and the Judge loitering far behind. There were so many people wandering in different directions, that the three groups were presently separated, and Alice and Lajos found themselves on a little eminence overlooking the village and the merry crowd below. A chorus of male voices was now lustily rendering "The Old Song of Tell," and the notes, softened by distance, rose sweetly from the valley. "How beautiful it all is!" Alice said; "but you do not seem to enjoy it; are you weary?"

"No; I wish we might walk on so for the rest of our lives. I am never tired with you. But now our paths separate for a time, and when I think of walking on alone I realize suddenly that I am a broken man, and that I am very weary."

Alice understood him, but showed no confusion. "Then you have decided to go to Italy?" she asked.

"Aunt has decided," he replied; "but we shall not remain long, and I shall join you at Baireuth before the Wagner festival is over. I hope we may have the pleasure of your company as we sail down the Danube. When do you return to your mission in Bulgaria?"

"The middle of next month; I have made a long vacation and am eager to return to my girls."

"Do you enjoy the work so very much?"

"So much, that it seems to me that philanthropy is the only thing worth living for."

COSTUME OF PEASANT OF UNTERWALDEN.

"I have come to think so, too. Tell me, Miss Alice, in what way can a man like me devote himself to his fellow-creatures? My career as a soldier was spoiled by that ugly wound, but I am not utterly disabled; I ought still to be able to do good and worthy work in the world in some fashion. Shall I turn missionary?"

"Think of your home," Alice replied; "is there no way that you can be a missionary to the people on your own estate, those for whom you are responsible, or are they all in such comfortable circumstances that they need to have nothing done for them?"

"The people of my own class need a good deal of evangelization, I fear; but there are the miners, the poor devils who work the lead mines, which give me my income. I have often thought of bettering their condition which I know is sad enough. If you will kindly visit my aunt on your way to Bulgaria, I will take you to the mines, and we will see what can be done for the miners and their families. The trouble is, that if I increase the miners' wages and lessen their hours of work, fit up their homes, establish a school and all that sort of thing, it will cost a great deal, and will really lessen my income. We are running these mines in close competition with other companies, and at a very small profit, and I must be careful or I shall throw myself out of the race entirely. It is as if I had inherited a plantation of slaves; emancipation to them means ruin to me."

"And yet can you hesitate?"

"No; I would not hesitate a moment if I were the only one concerned. Unfortunately, I am only half owner in the mines; the property of a ward of my uncle's is entangled in these mines, and I must give an account to her for my management of it. Again, if I ruin myself financially, how are the miners to live when I can no longer give them employment?"

"Can you not introduce reforms gradually, and make their lives a little more tolerable, if you cannot do all you wish at once?"

"Yes; I think I can. I do not need quite the amount which my aunt insists that I must obtain from the mines. I can give up the winter at Vienna for one thing; and this is why I want your opinion as to what it is best to do. That is, I shall want your opinion when I see you next, for then many things will be settled which are now in doubt. On the fifth of next August, by my uncle's will, there is to be a settlement of the estate. I shall then know just where I stand."

Alice looked at Lajos with keen disappointment. "Why does he not tell me," she thought, "that he is betrothed to his uncle's ward? Surely we are sufficiently intimate for such a confidence." But Lajos did not consider the disposal of his hand by his uncle's will as a valid betrothal. He had no intention of carrying out the conditions, and he was only impatient to see the young lady in order to make a satisfactory rendering to her of her property. His aunt and he had made every effort to find the missing heiress. They felt sure that the terms of the will must be known to her, and that she would probably be heard from by the fifth of August. If not, a certain portion of the property would be set aside and held subject to her demand, while Lajos would be free from all other obligations.

All of this passed through Lajos' mind, and seemed to make it advisable for him to make no formal proposal until he could ask Alice to help him make the best possible use of his fortune. If he were left a poor man he fancied that he had resolved never to marry. Still, chained as he was by circumstance, the opportunity was so tempting, he could not let her go from him with no assurance of his deep affection, and he added earnestly, "Trust me, Alice; wait for me until the time that I have set, and believe, meantime, whatever happens, that I love you devotedly."

Alice was deeply pained. It had seemed to Lajos that she must understand his position and be happy in the confidence that he would not rest until everything was satisfactorily arranged. But Alice did not understand. She looked him through and through with her clear, questioning eyes, and was dissatisfied. She believed his assurance that he loved her, but it brought her no comfort; for, if this were true, what more natural than that he should openly and honorably ask her hand in marriage? And since he had not done this, she felt convinced that the countess had told the truth, and that he was already betrothed. She longed frankly to ask him what it all meant, but he looked so true that she could not bring herself to tax him with double dealing. Besides, there was no longer any opportunity for confidential conversation. The girls were very near. "You make no comment, Alice, on my last remark."

She smiled faintly. "It does not seem to me that you have said a great deal."

"True enough," he replied, with a gay laugh. There was the least possible spice of pique in her remark, and it gave him the assurance which he wished. "Forget that I've said anything, until the fifth of August."

He called gayly to the others to join them, and the chat became general. It was evident that he had said more than he intended and that he wished no reply. He began to talk to Margaret about the wonderful engineering exhibited in the Axenstrasse, a magnificent

RAILWAY UP THE RIGI.

road which starts from Brunnen and joins the St. Gothard road at Altdorf.

The countess linked herself to Alice as they went down the hill, and kept her at her side until the day was over.

The friends were destined to pass only a few more golden days together. The ascent of the Rigi was the brightest of these, with a glorious view from its summit, but this has been so frequently described by other travellers that we shall omit an account of it here.

Margaret now felt that her visit to her aunt could not longer be postponed, and as the Judge was quite ready, the two announced their intention of proceeding to Zermatt.

The countess immediately decided that she would enjoy a short sojourn at The Riffel in view of the grandest peaks of Switzerland. She affected to be influenced by a wish to see the Matterhorn, which Lajos had formerly expressed, though he now assured her that he would rather do this at some other time, and that he had a strong desire to attend the Wagner festival at Baireuth.

"Ah! Wagner, Wagner!" replied the countess in a pet. "Who is it cares for Wagner! You sall let ze stove-pipe fall, and make one great explosion of dynamite in a shop of copper kettles, and you sall enjoy ze music of Wagner. You show me zoze who prefer it to ze Italian opera and I show you some imbeciles."

As Cecilia and Alice had just explained that they were devotees of Wagner on their way to the festival, the remarks of aunt and nephew were equally significant.

There was genuine regret in the parting of the girls. Cecilia and Margaret had made an appointment to meet again at the Fête of the Vignerons at Vevey, and to return to America together, but Alice would go on to her work in that strange land so far from our knowledge and thought, and they might never meet again. Margaret had felt herself strongly drawn to her, and she admired her devotion and self-sacrifice without having the slightest desire to emulate it.

The countess and Lajos with the Judge and Margaret now followed down the valley of the Rhone to the Visp. From this point the scenery became very wild and rugged, a great contrast to the majestic but quiet beauty of the Lucerne region. At length the grand obelisk of the Matterhorn (called also Monte Cervin and Monte Silvio) rose defiantly before them like a milestone of eternity.

"To think of any one having the temerity to climb that mountain!" exclaimed Lajos; "where is there the least crevice for the lodgment of human foot?"

"It cannot be as inaccessible as it appears," replied the Judge, "since it has been climbed; perhaps the other side is not so steep. This is a very good point of view for a photograph, however." And as he secured his negative, the old Judge fell in love with the mountain which has lured so many adventurous climbers on to their destruction. "I am rather glad that we are to stay in this neighborhood for some time," he said to himself. "I shall find an opportunity before we leave to ascend that mountain, and there will be a fact worthy of the summer." It was an access of his old malady of *mania scandens*, which Margaret had fancied was cured, and which was still destined to give her grave anxiety. The party were unusually silent; for it was necessary to proceed much of the way in single file, and every one was occupied wth his own thoughts. The countess was absorbed in conjectures respecting Margaret's relatives. "It is fortunate," she thought, "that I shall be

THE COMFORTS OF DONKEY-RIDING.

able to see them for myself. She is probably well connected, and if so, and if this niece of mine never appears, there shall be further intercourse between these Lochwalders and myself."

They reached the Riffel Hotel in time for an early dinner, and found Annette, who had come in to inquire if they had arrived. The

Judge, weary with his ride, counselled a halt until the next morning; but Margaret was impatient to find her aunt at the Alm or summer pasturage. "I will go on this afternoon with Annette, grandpa, and we will send a guide to bring you, with the luggage, in the morning."

A couple of donkeys were obtained at the hotel for the short journey; and they struck into a wild gorge, and followed the course of a little stream, which brawled over a rocky bed. It was the famous Zmvtthal, which has been described in the following graphic manner by a well-known traveller: —

"Three mountain-glens unite at Zermatt to form the valley of the Visp. Two are occupied by glaciers — great ice streams which, sweeping down on either side of the Riffelberg, drain the amphitheatre of peaks dominated by Monte Rosa. The other glen, however, called the Zmvtthal, extends into the mountains for a distance of about six miles, before the foot of the glacier is reached, between the base of the Matterhorn on one side and of the Gabehorn on the other. Paths exist on either side of the stream, which wind gently up and down through noble pine woods, among the usual combinations of boulders and rhododendrons, brushwood and fern, Alpine flowers and mosses, among which creep and cling the great serpent-like roots of the pines. The torrent roars in the ravine below, dashing, at one place, through a magnificent gorge, which is spanned by a frail bridge."

The character of the scenery had totally changed. The loveliness of the lake was replaced by the sublime grandeur of stern snow-peaks and savage passes, which seemed to tell of heroic adventure and endurance in the lives of the inhabitants of the region. Margaret felt the stimulating influence of the surroundings.

"An entirely new stage setting," she said. "Evidently a new act in the drama is to be ushered in. I wonder what it will be."

CHAPTER VIII.

OUR LADY OF POVERTY.

> She knew
> She was not wise; was conscious in herself
> Of eager impulses that would have wrecked
> Her whole heart's happiness a thousand times,
> Had not some Power from without herself
> Shut down the sudden gates, and with its stern
> "*Thou shalt not!*" left her stunned, perhaps, but saved.
> * * * * * * * *
> How could she help
> Believe that God had stooped from highest heaven
> To save her from herself.
> ALICE WELLINGTON ROLLINS.

MARGARET had felt a subtle premonition of the change which was coming, as mariners feel the chill in the atmosphere which announces the presence of an iceberg; but she was far from guessing the depth of poverty in which she would find her false relatives plunged.

"Annette," she said, as they rode on together, "I feel certain that you found my aunt in reduced circumstances. Is it not so?"

Annette nodded grimly.

"I want to know something about her before I see her. Do not be afraid of shocking me."

Annette, now that her revenge was within her grasp, was afraid to take it. "She will leave us in a storm of rage, and that will be the end of it," she thought. "It will be worth much to see her fury, but all money advantage to us will then be lost. It would be harder for her to have her humiliation come upon her by degrees. I think I will adopt that plan," and she replied, aloud: —

"Your great-aunt has one son, a widower, who lives with her with his two children. You would call them poor, but they consider themselves well off. You will not care to visit long with them, but you can help them if you really care to do so."

Up, up, up. They had left the Zmutt Thal and were climbing the slope of one of the northern ranges.

"There is a fine view of the Matterhorn and the southern mountains from the edge of that cliff," Annette said. "If you like, I will hold your donkey and you can dismount and get it."

Margaret walked to the edge of the precipice which Annette had indicated. Off to the south beautiful Italy was buried from her view by a barrier of stern mountain ranges, and she felt that the life of luxury to which she was accustomed was shut from her as well. For a moment there was a wild yearning for the past, and a sinking of heart in view of the future. If she could have gone back she would; for she stood upon the brink of a precipice more dangerous than the actual one before her. But she realized

ON THE BRINK OF A PRECIPICE.

that it was too late; and she looked up at the gigantic Matterhorn so startlingly near. More than ever it seemed to her a milestone of eternity, grim and terrible; but as she looked, the sunset flush transformed it into a thing of exquisite beauty. The deep rosy tint on the summit

THE MATTERHORN.

grew more and more delicate until it was lost in the snowy white of the sides, which again deepened into the cool green tints of the shadows near the base. It seemed a colossal crystal of tourmaline in its wonderful play of delicious color. Margaret was so absorbed in the spectacle that Annette called her twice before her attention was aroused. She came slowly away, all her nobler nature aroused by the glorious spectacle. "Life may be stern here," she thought, "but it must be heroic;" and the lines,

"Better not be at all than not be noble,"

flashed through her mind.

"I wonder if it is in me to do anything really grand," she thought. "If my aunt is poor I will share her life, and see how these peasants really live. I should not wonder if her simple pleasures were really more enjoyable than the *ennui* of the rich."

Something which she had read of the lives of the Swiss came to her mind, at this juncture. "Good, kind people, poetically minded, delight themselves in imagining the happy life led by peasants, who dwell by Alpine fountains. The time will come when, as the heavy folded curtain falls upon our stage of life, we shall begin to comprehend that the felicity we sympathized in was intended to have been bestowed." "Well," she thought, in answer to the admonition, "if my aunt is not comfortable I will try to make her so. I am ashamed that I have consulted my own selfish pleasure and have delayed coming to her for so long, but I will try to do my duty all the more faithfully now." It was the beginning of a new life, indeed, for Margaret.

Annette had prepared her more thoroughly than she knew for the ordeal before her, and Margaret had need of the preparation. The sun had set when they paused at the door of a rude châlet. The firelight gleamed within, and an old woman stood in the door peering out into the darkness. Dogs barked as they approached, and two children came bounding down the rocky path to meet them.

"Go away, Nikolas; off with you, Katchen!" Annette exclaimed, roughly shaking her bridle, which one of them had grasped. A man rose heavily from a bench in front of the house, and held the donkeys while they dismounted.

"*Ist es wirhlich du!*" exclaimed the old woman, "*Mein schatz, kind meines bruders?*" (Is it really thou, my treasure, child of my brother?) Her face, though old and homely, showed so much real delight that Margaret responded to her caresses by kissing her wrinkled cheek.

"This is thy cousin Yakob, named for thy grandfather, my loved brother," the old woman continued, indicating the stolid-looking peasant who held the donkeys, "and these are his children; but come in, come in, for I thought not to see thee in my poor house."

It was indeed a poor house, like most cow-keepers' châlets, occupied only as a summer cottage while the animals were pastured on the heights. Mother Lochwalder had a more comfortable and better-stocked home in Zermatt where she passed her winters, but it did not seem worth while to her to bring her household goods, the tall clock, the best carved bedstead, the porcelain stove, the spinning-wheel, and the stores of linen and pewter, on mule back up the mountains, to their summer camping ground. Consequently the furnishings of the first floor of the châlet, which was one great room, were of the simplest kind. The châlet was built on a side hill, and the cow-stable and milk-room occupied the basement. A fourth of the area of the living-room was filled with hay, and there was a hole in the floor through which it could be forked into the mangers. A rough stone hearth was built up on one side of the room, and here hung the great kettle used in heating the milk for cheese-making. Brightly scoured tin pans were ranged on a shelf near by, with a few cooking utensils of the rudest description. A large table with twisted legs stood in the centre of the room; Mother Lochwalder's second-best bedstead, piled high with feather beds, in the corner opposite the hay, and the cheese-press in another corner. A faint smell of sour milk and of smoke was diffused throughout the apartment; but the room was clean, and as the two doors and window were both open, the ventilation was good and the odors not positively unendurable. Margaret approached the fire and sat down upon a rude bench, overcome by the poverty of her aunt's surroundings. Annette watched her keenly, with malicious triumph in her expression. Mother Lochwalder bustled about, and placed on the table a china bowl of rich cream and a loaf of brown bread. Margaret ate mechanically, and as she was very hungry, the supper seemed delicious.

"Will you have tea, my treasure?" asked the old woman. "Annette said you never drank it, but I have some excellent green tea with which I indulge myself on Sundays. I have also a bottle of wine and some sausages. Speak the word and I will cook them for you — delicious little sausages. Katchen, bring the cheese!"

"Yes, aunt, I would like to taste the cheese if you made it, but never mind the sausages or the wine." Margaret spoke gently, and Mother Lochwalder bustled about greatly delighted; but the girl's mind was in a turmoil of rebellion and dismay. When the old woman's back was turned, a strange object which had been lying under the table, its head pillowed on the dog, crept out and approached Margaret on all fours. The girl uttered a shriek of fright; for in the dusk of the room, so hideous was the appearance of this unfortunate creature, dwarfed, with long, unkempt hair, one of its bare feet twisted inward, its clawlike fingers tapping her knee for recognition, that at first she fancied that it was a great baboon. What added greatly to this impression was the abnormally large ears which the dwarf had the power of flapping grotesquely. A second glance, and the sensation of fear gave place to one of loathing. That pale, old face was human indeed, but rendered hideous by frightful contortions. The dwarf continued to pat her knee, at the same time chattering incoherently.

"Oh! what is it?" Margaret exclaimed. "Take it away, take it away!"

Annette laughed unpleasantly. "That is your cousin Nikolas," she said. Her revenge was complete, and a world of exultation was expressed in her laugh. Tears were gathering in Margaret's eyes, and Annette doubted not that they were tears of rage and humiliation; but she did not know Margaret. After the first horrified surprise, a great wave of pity swept over the girl's heart. "Poor little thing," she said, as Mother Lochwalder led the child away; "can nothing be done for him? Is there no possible cure?"

"There are asylums, but they cost money," said Yakob, the child's father.

"I will pay for him," Margaret replied, promptly. "We will see about it at once."

Annette was rather surprised at this turn of affairs, but she said to herself, "Yes, indeed, my lady, you will pay for that and for much more before you leave us. We will make all we can out of your brief visit; for you want to get away from us as soon as you can. I see it in your eyes."

Margaret rose from the table. "I am very tired," she said, in a voice which trembled a little in spite of the strong control which she endeavored to place upon herself. "I think I had better bid you all good-night."

Annette lighted a candle, and led the way up a rude staircase, which was hardly more than a ladder, to the loft above. A partition across one end made a bed-room, wide enough, but so low that Margaret could only stand upright in the centre. The bed, with home-spun blue coverlet, looked clean and inviting. An earthen jug of fresh water and a brown earthenware bowl were placed on a box, which served as dressing-table. A coarse but clean towel lay beside it; but the place where one might have expected to find a mirror was filled by a gaudy print of the Virgin, Our Lady of Poverty. And this was all the furnishing which the room contained, with the exception of Margaret's hand-bag.

"Good-night, cousin," said Annette maliciously, as she placed the candle in the centre of the wash-bowl, and turned to leave the room.

The word stabbed through Margaret's stupor like a sword-thrust. "Cousin!" she exclaimed; "my cousin! Impossible!"

"I am the child of Yakob Lochwalder's sister. Your aunt is my grandmother. I am as nearly related to you as the rest," Annette replied doggedly.

This was the unkindest cut of all. Margaret had accepted the old peasant woman as her aunt; had accepted the poverty of the hut; had accepted even the poor dwarf; but Annette! — her whole nature revolted, and for the first time the old volcanic temper surged to the surface. She was ready to shriek, "It is a lie! I do not believe it. I never will recognize you as my cousin." By a strong effort she repressed the words; but she was too much agitated to make any other reply, and turning quickly, she walked to the window, pretending to look out into the night, but seeing nothing. Annette had expected an angry outburst, and was disappointed. Perhaps Margaret had not heard.

"Good-night, cousin," she said again; "since we are relatives, we should also be friends."

Margaret had partly recovered herself in that brief interval. "As true friends as relatives," she said, simply extending her hand. It was a chance remark, but it struck home. Did Margaret suspect?

In spite of her effrontery, Annette was cowed, and she left the room sullenly. Margaret waited only until Annette had descended the ladder to sink upon the bed and indulge in a passion of hysterical weeping. She was overwrought, physically and mentally; but sleep came presently, to unbend the strained faculties, and give her strength for the trials still to come.

When she awoke, the sun was shining through a hole in the wall, — it could hardly be called a window, — and the child Katchen was tapping at her door.

"Lady cousin, lady cousin," said Katchen, "I have brought you some edelweiss. Grandmother said you would like it."

Margaret rubbed her eyes, and for a moment could not realize the situation. It all came back to her with a glance at Our Lady of Poverty. "Come here, little girl," she said; "I want to look at you."

The child approached timidly. She was a pretty, flaxen-haired little creature, with eyes as blue as German forget-me-nots, and sturdy legs, red from paddling that morning in a mountain-brook. On the whole Margaret was pleased with her appearance.

KATCHEN.

"I foresee that we shall have fine times together, little Katchen," she said. "Will you take me to walk with you this morning?"

"Yes, heartily; but first you must come to breakfast. We have meat; for father killed a steinbock this morning. He says it is a sign that you have brought us luck, for they are rare — very rare — and he has not been able to shoot one before this season. They would give him ten dollars for it below at the hotel, but he says he will not sell his luck. Hurry, lady; do you not smell the meat frying? O blessed saints! is it not good?"

Margaret hastened her toilet, and was about to descend, but the child lingered. "What is it, Katchen?" she asked.

"Aren't you going to pray to Our Lady of Poverty before you go down?"

Margaret felt rebuked, and replied, "Yes, dear, I will pray, but not to Our Lady of Poverty. We will pray to the God of all riches, who is able to make us rich." And falling upon her knees, she asked for grace sufficient for that day, and even as she prayed received the answer; for Katchen softly opened the little window, and the rush of pure, cool air across her face seemed to her the swift sweeping of the wings of angels sent to strengthen her.

"Look at the mountain," Katchen said, as she rose from her knees; and Margaret noticed for the first time that the window framed a magnificent view of the Weisshorn — a shining crystal miracle in a circle of billowy clouds, the morning mists apparently cleft through by a wedge of transparent glass. Again there came to her the exuberant uplifting of soul which she had felt on the Wengern Alp.

YAKOB LOCHWALDER.

"I cannot fail to be noble in such noble surroundings," she thought; and twining an arm around Katchen, she joined the family below. Honest Yakob was smoking his porcelain pipe; but he shut down its silver lid with a snap as she approached. "Good morning, cousin," he said heartily. "My daughter Annette here says that our ways are not fine enough for you, but we have a breakfast this morning that is fit for a kaiser. I went hunting once with the grand duke of Baden, who was spending a summer at The Riffel. We had no such luck as this."

Mother Lochwalder laughed. "Yakob is always talking about that hunt with the grand duke," she said. "One would fancy that Yakob was one of the invited guests, when in reality he was only a pack animal like the other donkeys.

It is well said, one must never believe a *Jagdgeschichte* " (story of a huntsman).

Margaret expressed her appreciation and seated herself at the table as Katchen drew up a chair for her.

"Nay, come first without and see the creature's head. I have cut it off to take to Zermatt, to the taxidermist below there. He will mount it, and sell it to some traveller who will boast that he has killed the steinbock — the liar. It is not every one who is quick enough to bring down a creature like that, even if he has the luck to see him."

"Yes, take the head to the taxidermist," Margaret replied; "but do not sell it. My grandfather will be glad to buy it of you, and it will be glory enough for him to tell his friends that he has eaten a steak from the animal."

Nikolas stood outside the châlet looking at the head of the steinbock. The poor deformed creature was scarcely less repulsive by daylight than when Margaret had first seen him; but she repressed a shudder, and spoke to him kindly.

"Horns, horns," he said, pointing to the long, curving horns of the steinbock or ibex.

"He has some intelligence," Margaret exclaimed, eagerly; "he is not an utter cretin."

"Oh, no," replied the father; "mother will have it that he knows more than he can tell, but that he is bewitched, the unfortunate, by the same spell which killed his mother, who died when he was born. Better he had died and she had lived, for she was a good woman — my heart's love — my angel!"

Mother Lochwalder now appeared, and urged Margaret to take her breakfast, which she was very willing to do. The pleasant sunshine and bracing air gave a different aspect to the situation, and she felt herself better able to cope with it than the evening before. ·She gave only a distant nod to Annette, however, who wisely kept herself in the background. The meat of the steinbock was strong and tough, but she praised it, and assured Mother Lochwalder that her grandfather would be delighted to have some for dinner. "And now," she said, after the breakfast was over, "I do not want to be a burden to you while we stay, so you must let us pay our board as we would have to do anywhere else."

"Annette said you would not want to stay long," Yakob replied in surprise, while Annette herself drew near and listened wonderingly.

"This is just the region for my grandfather; he determined before we set out on this journey that he would like to do some mountaineering in the neighborhood of Zermatt. He is not fit to climb mountains; but if you can guide him where it is safe for him to go, it will be a great pleasure to him, and a great relief to me, and he will pay you well for it."

A look of great delight passed over Yakob's countenance. "My father was a guide before me and his brother, your other grandfather, was also a guide, none better in Switzerland. I, too, am qualified to be a guide; for I have twice climbed the Matterhorn; but no one has ever hired me, no one would trust me after my uncle" — he hesitated — "after my uncle went to America. And so the nearest I ever came to being a guide was when the grand duke's huntsman engaged me to drive the pack mule that was to carry the game. Heillige Johannis! but it was a light load altogether! But now if I am seen guiding a rich American, and carrying him safely through the season, it will be a start in business for me for the rest of my life."

The honest fellow's happiness was pleasant to see. "And now," continued Margaret, "as I promised my grandfather to send for him this morning, we must settle on what provision we can make for his comfort. As he will be out of doors nearly all the time, his wants will be simple. He will be satisfied with my little bed-room under the roof, with the few additions which I can easily make, if you can tuck me away somewhere else. Can I not share Annette's room?"

Annette uttered an exclamation of astonishment. Was it possible that this proud girl had come to this, and that she was willing to room with her former serving-maid? So thunderstruck was she, that she did not reply. Margaret thought that she was offended by her coldness on the preceding evening, and her impulsive nature, which would never permit her to do anything by halves, prompted her to say, "I think you will find me more agreeable, Cousin Annette, than in our old relations."

"But you cannot sleep together," said Mother Lochwalder, "for Annette and Katchen sleep with me, and three in one bed are enough. We have no rooms but those you have seen. Yakob and Nikolas sleep on the hay in the corner."

"Perhaps your grandfather would be more comfortable at the hotel in the valley," Yakob suggested.

"I do not like to have him away from me," Margaret explained. "Can I not hire furniture enough to fit up the other end of the loft as a bed-room?"

"We have furniture in plenty at the house in Zermatt," said Mother Lochwalder. "Annette, go down with thy father and see that a cart is loaded with my best carved bedstead and plenty of bedding, and all other things necessary, and bring it up this very day."

"Good," said Yakob, "we will start immediately, and Katchen, you must help your grandmother mind the cows while I am gone. I will bring back a herds-boy from the village that I may be the freer to tramp it with his excellency."

They set out at once, the head of the steinbock — a trophy of which Yakob was very proud — hanging over his shoulder.

When they had gone, Mother Lochwalder took down her alpenstock and her knitting, and went out to watch the cows, grumbling a little to herself as she went that if it were not for this duty she would scrub the floor of the living-room, and make all more fitting for the reception of the gracious gentleman who was to be their guest.

"What must be done for the cows? Can I do it?" Margaret asked.

"Simply to sit in the pasture yonder, and watch that none of them stray, or break into the enclosed yard where the fodder is kept. If any of them attempt to do this, call me, and I will come and help you."

Margaret took the alpenstock and sat down on a stone in a corner of the pasture. About twenty cows and a dozen calves were feeding within a short distance. In her heart she was a miserable coward, but she tried to assume a courageous aspect. Katchen was in a talkative mood, and told over the names of the cows. "That is Brown Velvet," said Katchen, pointing to a beautiful young creature with a hide like black plush brindled with fawn-color. "She wears the silver bell, and she knows that she is princess. All the others follow her, and none of them would dare to take the lead, nor would the others follow a cow that did not wear the bell. You should see the cows when they set out for the Alm in the early summer. The instant the collars are placed on their necks they understand, and range themselves in order of procession, and it is just so when we leave the Alm in the fall to return to the valley."

"But there are other cows wearing bells," Margaret remarked.

"Yes, but only one silver bell. Listen; its tinkle is different from the rest, and as it is larger, the sound is louder and clearer. The other bells are all tuned to chime with the leader's. Grandmother paid thirty dollars for the set. See the beautiful red embroidery on the collars!"

"If all the other cows follow the leader, I should think it would be very important that she should be a well-behaved creature, not given to gadding about."

"She is, and so teachable, at the first sound of the yodel she will leave the richest clover, and follow. Nikolas, yodel for our lady cousin, and show her how Brown Velvet will come!"

"Pray, do not!" Margaret exclaimed. "I had much rather she would stay where she is."

"Nikolas can yodel so beautifully," said Katchen. "You must

hear him some day, but he is afraid to do it unless he is told to; for once he led the cows into a distant ravine and gave father trouble to find them."

Nikolas sprang from the ground and went through the pantomime of yodelling without uttering a sound.

"Not now, good Nikolas," Margaret entreated. The strange creature replied with many uncouth contortions, and, turning a handspring, capered away toward the other side of the pasture.

"Ought we not to watch him and keep him from straying as well as the cows?" Margaret asked.

"Nikolas? Oh, no! he goes where he will, and he is never lost. Do see him now! he has climbed that tree like a squirrel."

They chatted on for a little while, when Margaret was startled by a low bellowing, and looking up saw a huge bull between them and the châlet, and trotting directly toward them. "O Katchen!" she exclaimed, "what shall we do?"

"It is Schreckhorn who has got out of his pen. Run, run!" shouted Katchen, suiting the action to the word; but Margaret was paralyzed with terror, and could not move. She did not notice that the bull was attracted not by herself, but by Brown Velvet who was quietly feeding just beyond her. On came the bull, when suddenly, clear and distinct across the pasture, like the warbling of some strange bird, sounded the yodel. Brown Velvet shook her silver bell and trotted in the direction of Nikolas, who had scrambled down out of his tree and skipped along with many strange antics, yodelling as he went. The bull turned abruptly and followed Brown Velvet, and Margaret, restored to the possibility of action by her release, ran quickly to the châlet. Mother Lochwalder, mop in hand, ran to the pasture and succeeded in getting the bull inside the pen which he had quitted; but Margaret was too much unstrung to watch the cows any longer that day. She believed that Nikolas had seen her danger and had yodelled with the intention of drawing away the bull. Her gratitude was excited, and her respect for his intelligence heightened. "He is not idiotic, I am sure of that," she said to herself, and when he came into the châlet she called him to her and tried to draw him into conversation. But he was either more wanting than she had thought, or else he was wilfully perverse; for he would not reply, but retired to his favorite resting-place under the table, and sat there nursing his knees, with the dancing firelight reflected in his eyes, till they glowed like coals, and he reminded her of one of the little mountain gnomes which the Germans love to imagine.

The next event of the day, which followed almost immediately, was the arrival of her grandfather. He did not come on foot with Yakob, as she had anticipated, but in a carriage, and accompanied by the countess and Lajos. Margaret had not expected a visit from them. She fancied that she had parted from her friends finally the night before. Indeed, so much emotion and such an entirely new range of experience had been crowded into the past twenty-four hours, that she could hardly realize that it was only on the preceding afternoon that she had left the countess at the Riffel Hotel.

A GOATHERD OF THE ZERMATT VALLEY.

The countess raised her lorgnette as she entered the châlet, and looked about her with undisguised scorn.

"So this is your aunt's abode!" she exclaimed in good German, abandoning her attempts at English, as she always did when greatly excited. "And where is the lady?"

"She is herding the cows in the pasture," Margaret replied, holding her head very high, and fearing that the countess might mistake the flush of indignation on her cheeks for a blush of shame.

"So—a fine accomplishment, indeed!" Yakob entered the house, and hung his hat above his gun. "And is that boor also related to you?"

"He is my cousin."

The countess laughed in a disagreeable manner. "And why, when you conferred upon us the honor of your acquaintance, did you not inform us of the distinguished station of your honorable family?"

"I did not know it myself, madame."

"A likely story."

"If my relatives and their home displease you, may I be permitted to remind you, madame, that you are an uninvited guest?"

"Highty, tighty! But I like you the better for standing up for your people. Merciful heavens, what have we here?" Nikolas had crept from under the table, and was feeling of the countess's robe, as he had felt of Margaret's the night before. "What, is it a family of idiots? Take the loathsome creature away!" It was only twenty-four hours since Margaret had been moved by a similar impulse of revolt, but she sprang now to the boy's side, and led him tenderly away from the countess, lifting the slight, misshapen figure to a seat beside her on the hearth. "My cousin Nikolas is deformed, but he is not an idiot," she said. "He was quick-witted enough this morning to save my life, and I should be base not to love him for it."

"Ah! you mean that I have forgotten that you saved my life."

"No, madame, I had forgotten it myself; besides, it was not I, but Alice, who did it."

"There, there, don't get angry. One would think you belonged to my family by the way you fly into a temper. It is no fault of yours, child, that your relatives are not presentable. I like you, and I have a proposition to make to you. Give them a little money. Buy from

them a promise that they will never trouble you again. Cut yourself
loose from them, and I will adopt you; for I have given up all hope of
finding my friend's niece. You shall take her place in my heart and
my fortune. Come! I am a fiery-tempered old lady, but I love you.
That is your aunt, I presume, with the pail of swill. Which of us do
you prefer?"

There was a yearning tenderness in the countess's voice, which
moved Margaret in spite of her indignation.

"Pardon me, dear countess, but it is not a matter of preference,"
she replied, kindly. "We do not choose our relatives. God gives
them to us and us to them. I thank you more than I can tell, but this
is my place, and I must stay here."

"I said well that it was a family of idiots," exclaimed the countess.
"I believe you are an idiot yourself. Lajos, your arm. Conduct me to
the carriage."

Lajos obeyed, and Margaret thought that he too had cast her off;
but a moment afterward he returned.

"Miss Margaret," he said, respectfully, "allow me to assure you of
my profound admiration."

"And gratitude?" Margaret added, mischievously, though the tears
trembled on her lashes. "Are you so glad that I did not accept the
countess's offer?"

"No, truly. I wish with all my heart that we had any one in our
family so truly noble. Can you not come with us now, and later
explain everything?"

"No, Lajos, I cannot repudiate my relatives."

"Good by, then, friend Margaret. I am proud to call you so."

"Good by, friend Lajos."

The Judge, who had been listening in an utterly dazed manner,
now asked Margaret to explain what it all meant. Margaret did so,
and he assumed a judicial expression. "As between the plaintiff, the
honorable Countess de Krajova and the defendant cow-keeperess

Lochwalder," he said, stroking his beard with a sly twinkle in his gray eyes. "As between the claims of these ladies, the court, without having seen the said cow-keeperess, renders its decision in favor of the defendant; for," he added, "that countess is a vixen and any variety of woman-kind would be pleasanter as a relative."

Mother Lochwalder entered at this juncture and was duly presented, but as the Judge could not speak German or Mother Lochwalder English, their greetings were confined to bows and curtsies.

While Mother Lochwalder was preparing dinner, Margaret told her grandfather of the head of the steinbock which had been sent away to be mounted for him. She led him out upon the balcony, and made him admire the superb view, and even ventured with him into the cow-yard where Yakob was milking, showed him Brown Velvet and the chime of silver bells and told him of the adventure of the day. Then they went in to supper and the worthy man enjoyed a piece of broiled steinbock followed by Swiss cheese, coffee and marmalade — "a dinner fit for a king!" he declared.

Shortly after, Annette appeared before the châlet with an ox-cart loaded with household furniture, and the remainder of the eventful day was employed in converting the loft into a bed-room for the Judge.

The good man was delighted with everything. "It is like roughing it in the Rockies," he confided to Margaret, "and will make a capital episode in my lecture."

CHAPTER IX.

LIFE AT THE ALM.

Here it may well seem to the traveller if there be sometimes hardships, there must be at least innocence and peace, and fellowship of the human soul with nature. It is not so. The wild goats that leap along those rocks have as much passion of joy in all that fair work of God, as the men that toil among them; perhaps more. They do not understand so much as the name of beauty or of knowledge. They understand dimly that of virtue. Love, patience, hospitality, faith — these things they know. To glean their meadows side by side, so happier; to bear the burden up the breathless mountain flank unmurmuringly; to bid the stranger drink from their vessel of milk; to see at the foot of their low death-beds a pale figure upon a cross dying also patiently, — in this they are different from the cattle and the stones. — RUSKIN.

MARGARET began at once to assist in the regular home work at the Châlet. There was plenty to be done. While Yakob, having performed the morning milking, was away on long tramps with the Judge, it was necessary that some one should watch the cows, and as Margaret had had enough of this occupation, Annette usually undertook it, and Margaret relieved Mother Lochwalder by making the cheese, while Katchen did the morning churning. There were so many operations in the cheese-making, that it occupied nearly all the forenoon. A trap-door led from the living-room to the milk-room which opened from the stable. The Judge had been their guest but a few days before he showed Yakob how to conduct a stream of water from a neighboring brook through the dairy, making a cool canal in which the milk-pans could stand, and to lead it after it had done this service into a trough in front of the noses of the cattle so as to do away with the drudgery of bringing water to them. The Judge was much amused by their primitive methods of carrying on their work, and was constantly inventing and suggesting labor-saving machines. It was a difficult feat to climb the ladder from the dairy with a milk-pan in one's hands, and after Margaret had spilled several, the Judge constructed a rude dumb-waiter, by which the milk could be hoisted to a height from which it could be easily poured into the great cauldron, into which it must be warmed before it could be converted into Swiss cheese. Mother Lochwalder would then put in the rennet, and Margaret would stir it continually for half an hour when it would be curdled, and could be strained and the curds put in the press. Then the whey must be carried out to the pigs, and the churn, milk-pails, and pans washed and scoured. All of this Margaret took upon herself, while Mother Lochwalder performed the other household duties. Then there was the task of turning the heavy cheeses and rubbing them with salt, and after that her labor for the day was over. Annette had brought up the spinning-wheel with the other furniture from Zermatt, and after their noonday meal Mother Lochwalder would sit in front of the house and spin, while Katchen would knit interminable stockings. Margaret chose this time to instruct the children. She found that Nikolas had one talent of no mean order. Among Mother Lochwalder's treasures was a fine zither; on this Nikolas would play by the hour, pouncing upon the strings with his misshapen clawlike fingers and bringing out weird strains, imitations of the wind and of the cries of birds. On Sundays there were generally visitors at the Alm; their nearest neighbors from other pastures, or old friends from Zermatt. Frequently a musician was found among them who would touch the zither while the others sang the Alpine ballads. A plaintive one was the farewell to the Alm.

> "Farewell to the pastures
> So sunny and bright;
> The herdsman must leave you
> When summer takes flight.
>
> "We shall come to the mountains again, when the voice
> Of the cuckoo is heard, bidding all things rejoice;

When the earth dons her fairest and freshest array,
And the streamlets are flowing in beautiful May.

"To pastures and meadows,
 Farewell, then, once more!
The herdsman must go,
 For the summer is o'er."

During the singing of these songs Nikolas would sit spellbound, and after the visitors had departed would often reproduce them in part upon the zither. One day Margaret thought of the music-box which her grandfather had purchased in Geneva, and she set it in motion before Nikolas. It really seemed as if the little fellow would go wild with delight. He hugged it in his arms, and capered and danced; then carried it under the table, and lay down with it beneath his head. Very patiently Margaret set herself to teach him some of the rudiments of music. She was able to hire a poor piano in Zermatt, and she had it brought to the châlet and placed near the cheese-press.

YAKOB ACCEPTS HIS RELATIVES.

It was a difficult task, but she never wearied; for she felt sure of ultimate success. Annette, though apparently absorbed in her embroidery-frame and in tending the cows, watched her narrowly. She had not had the pleasure of seeing Margaret betrayed into a single exhibition of temper; and she could not help feeling that she was thwarted in her revenge, while she wondered what had come over the girl, and still regarded her with cold suspicion and hatred.

"I tell you," Yakob had said, when alone with his daughter, "I heard her, with my own ears, refuse the offer of that great lady to be taken away with her, and to be adopted as her niece."

"What!" exclaimed Annette. "Did she refuse to be the niece of the countess? And for what reason?"

"Because, as she said, she preferred to share the lot of her own people. Ah! blood is stronger than water. She has proved herself a true Lochwalder. I did not think, from what you said, that I would like her or her grandfather; but they are as good as any of us. So here's to them, say I," and lifting a huge porcelain tankard of beer to his lips, he drained it to the dregs in honor of his new relations.

A feeling of shame came over Annette for the first time. So long as she was sure that Margaret would revolt at the relationship, and disown it if possible, she had felt no compunction for her deception; but that she should accept the situation so sweetly was something utterly beyond her conception, and it grew more and more galling as the days went on.

No better guide could have been found for the erratic Judge than Yakob Lochwalder. He took him on trips suited to his strength,— on short and easy ones at first,— or else prevailed upon him to make the longer expeditions on mule-back. For a time, the Judge enjoyed these safe excursions immensely; but after a time they failed to satisfy him. The Matterhorn was always before him, exercising the same fateful fascination which it had wielded over so many unfortunate travellers. It was in vain that he was told of the accidents which had occurred to experienced mountaineers while vainly attempting its ascent. He was madly bent upon it. The summit had been really attained by Mr. Edward Whymper, and the Judge insisted on following his example.

In her endeavor to disenchant her grandfather Margaret read him one evening Mr. Whymper's account of his repeated trials and his final ascent, at once so successful and so disastrous, since they succeeded at the expense of the death of four of the party. No description of the Matterhorn gives so perfect an idea of its charm and its danger as this thrilling story, and we insert it here:—

"We started," says Edward Whymper, "from Zermatt on the 13th of July, 1865, at half-past five on a perfectly cloudless morning. We were eight in number. [Lord Francis Douglas, Messrs. Hudson, Hadow, and Whymper, and the guides, Michel Croz and Peter Taugwalder and his son.] On the first day we did not intend to ascend to any great height, and we mounted very leisurely. At half-past eleven we arrived at the base of the actual peak. Before twelve we had found a good position for the tent at a height of eleven thousand feet. Long after dusk the cliffs echoed with our laughter and the songs of the guides.

"We assembled together outside the tent before dawn on the morning of the 14th, and started directly it was light. On turning to the eastern face, the whole of the great slope was revealed, rising for three thousand feet, like a huge natural staircase.

"At 9.55 we arrived at the foot of that part which from Zermatt seems perpendicular or overhanging, and could no longer continue on the eastern side. By common consent we turned to the right or northern side. The work became difficult, and required caution. The general slope of the mountain was less than forty degrees; and snow had accumulated in it, and filled the interstices of the rock face, leaving only occasional fragments projecting here and there. These were at times covered with a thin film of ice. This solitary, difficult part was of no great extent. A long stride around a rather awkward corner brought us to snow once more. The last doubt vanished. The Matterhorn was ours! Croz now took the tent-pole, and planted it in the highest snow. 'Yes,' we said, 'there is the flagstaff; but where is the flag?' 'Here it is,' he answered, pulling off his blouse, and fixing it to the stick. It made a poor flag; and there was no wind to float it out, yet it was seen all around. They saw it at

Zermatt, at The Riffel, in the Val Tournache. At Breuil the watchers cried, 'Victory is ours!'

"We remained on the summit for one hour,—'one crowded hour of glorious life.' It passed away too quickly, and we began to prepare for the descent.

"We agreed that it would be best for Croz to go first, and Hadow second; Hudson, who was almost equal to a guide, wished to be third; Lord F. Douglas was placed next, and old Peter Taugwalder, the strongest of the remainder, after him. A few minutes later I tied myself to young Peter, ran down after the others, and caught them just as they were commencing the descent of the difficult part. Great care was being taken, only one man moving at a time. Lord F. Douglas asked me to tie on to old Peter, as he feared that he would not be able to hold his ground if a slip occurred. No one was actually descending when Mr. Hadow slipped, fell against Croz, and knocked him over. I heard one startled exclamation from Croz, then saw him and Mr. Hadow flying downward. In another moment Hudson was dragged from his steps, and Lord F. Douglas immediately after him. All this was the work of a moment. Immediately we heard Croz's exclamation, old Peter and I planted ourselves as firmly as the rocks would permit. The rope was taut between us, and the jerk came on us both as on one man. We held, but the rope broke midway between Taugwalder and Lord Francis Douglas. For a few seconds we saw our unfortunate companions sliding downward on their backs, and spreading out their hands, endeavoring to save themselves. They passed from our sight uninjured, disappeared one by one, and fell from precipice to precipice on to the Matterhorn gletscher below, a distance of nearly four thousand feet in height. From the moment the rope broke it was impossible to help them. For more than two hours afterward I thought every moment that the next would be my last; for the Taugwalders, utterly unnerved, were not only incapable of giving assistance, but were in such a state that a slip might have been

THE ACCIDENT ON THE MATTERHORN.

expected from one or the other at any moment. Immediately on my arrival at Zermatt I sent to the President of the Commune, and requested him to send as many men as possible to ascend heights, whence the spot could be commanded where I knew the four must have fallen. By 8.30 Sunday morning we had got within sight of the corner, in which we knew my companions must be. As we saw one weather-beaten man after another raise the telescope, turn deadly pale, and pass it on without a word to the next, we knew that all hope was gone."

The bodies of the unfortunate men, with the exception of Lord Francis Douglas, were recovered and buried at Zermatt.

Margaret translated the account into German for the benefit of Mother Lochwalder. "Ah, yes!" she said, "I remember that expedition well, and how every one said, 'This will put an end to the foolish risking of life in attempting to climb the mountain.' But, no; there were more attempts than ever. The young men of Zermatt were crazy to say that they had accomplished it, and not the young men only, but the young women also; and Theresa Carrel, the daughter of a noted guide, really got to the top. I warrant you she had offers of marriage in plenty after that. Then Professor Tyndal, who was often in the valley, and had tried it time and time again, would not be beaten by this Mr. Whymper, and at last he succeeded. And then some Italians gained the summit from the south. And after that every dandy who came into the valley with an alpenstock must needs try; but only one out of a hundred succeeds, though they have cut out a path and fastened chains along the face of that slippery rock where the mountaineers you read of met their death. But look you, it is no pleasure excursion still. Tell your grandfather to be warned by us, and not to attempt it; for this family has woful cause to dread the Matterhorn. It was fleeing from the revenge of the Matterhorn that your other grandfather, my brother, went to America; and now it seems as if the mountain had drawn one of your family back by an evil spell to wreak its doom upon him."

"How was it, Mother Lochwalder?" Margaret asked. "I have

often wondered what caused my grandfather Lochwalder to leave Switzerland, and I wish you would tell me the story."

The old woman seemed inclined to comply, but Yakob spoke up. "There is no need of distressing her with that old scandal," he said to his mother. "Your grandfather, my uncle, was an honest man," he added, speaking to Margaret. "It matters not what others say to the contrary. Ask no more, for you will get only lies and sorrow for your pains."

"I am glad that you can assure me that there is no stain on my grandfather's honor," Margaret replied. "So long as we know that he did only what was right it is no matter what others may say of him."

No one replied, and Margaret left the room. As she did so, Annette remarked significantly, "What did I tell you! She is proud, proud to the core. It is well you did not tell her the truth. She would have dropped us as if we were offal if you had done so."

Margaret was of course only the more keenly anxious to hear the entire story, but she restrained her curiosity for the time, sure that it would all come out in the end. For many days she puzzled over the mystery which connected the emigration of her supposed Grandfather Lochwalder with the Matterhorn, without coming to any satisfactory result. But one afternoon she thought that she had discovered the solution in a story of Katchen's. Much that was weird and supernatural was connected with the mountain by popular tradition, and Katchen told her many fairy tales of gnomes and elves that inhabited its caves. The child informed her gravely that the top of the mountain was only a step lower than heaven, and that, before it had been climbed by mortal foot, the spirits of all good people who had died in Zermatt and the regions round had preferred to make their residence here in sight of their old homes rather than go quite away from their dear ones, and that the top of the mountain had been fitted up as a Paradise for them. "The streams were bridged with long loaves of bread, the paths paved with cheeses, the cracks in the rocks plastered with butter, and people amused themselves with playing nine-pins with balls made of cheese and pins of butter." So said the child, and she firmly believed, not only that holy men and women attained this Paradise, but also that the gentlest and most faithful animals were, at their death, transported thither. "Brown Velvet would have gone there," she was sure, if the sanctuary had remained inviolate. Old chamois hunters had said that sometimes they had seen herds of wonderfully beautiful chamois sporting on the sides of the mountain, and when they had shot at them the leaden bullets rebounded from their sides as though they were bonbons, and the chamois spread out delicate wings, spotted like those of butterflies, and floated away to the summit.

Herds of spirit cows, too, whose bells played celestial tunes, had been sometimes seen by adventurous herdsmen, who had mounted nearly to the top. One of these had been caught, her father had told her, by some relative of theirs, and had been brought to the Alm. It had escaped after a time, and undoubtedly made its way back to the mountain, but had left behind it a calf, which had been reared, and had become a very beautiful heifer, taking the prize at all of the fairs. This animal had in its turn disappeared on one moonlight night, when the trap-door had been left open in the kitchen floor. It was Yakob's belief that the creature had unfolded wings, like those of the spirit chamois, and had flown straight up through the kitchen chimney to the magic mountain. Brown Velvet was a descendant of this wonderful creature, and it was Katchen's fear that the beautiful animal might sometime develop her butterfly wings and soar away, and she frequently stroked Brown Velvet's sides to see if the wings were budding.

Margaret reminded the child of her grandmother's saying, that a huntsman's stories are not to be believed, and then wondered if this were not the crime on the Matterhorn committed by her grandfather, for which he had fled the country. It seemed absurd that so childish a fable should be believed by grown people, and yet they were all singularly childlike, and she determined to ask Mother Lochwalder about it that evening. An event occurred that day which, while it was connected with this fairy tale, was so startling and terrible, that all curiosity in regard to her dead grandfather was blotted out by her anxiety for her living one.

The story of Mr. Whymper's ascent had the same effect on the Judge as its first recital had had upon the fraternity of Alpine climbers — he was all the more eager to attempt the Matterhorn; Yakob manifested fortunately a great reluctance to undertake it. He had made the ascent, and he knew the difficulties were too great for the Judge; moreover, he had a superstitious fear of the Matterhorn's revenge — some fatality to come to himself from the undertaking. He consequently continued to tempt the Judge to make many another excursion, to shoot chamois in the Einfisch Valley, to look for crystals along the edge of the glacier, and to trudge over the Theodule Pass into Italy. This last was a favorite scheme of Yakob's, and the Judge had given it his approval. "I will go around to Mont Blanc that way, Lochwalder," he had said, "but that will be after I have exhausted Zermatt and conquered the Matterhorn."

Margaret sighed. "If Mr. Walker were only here!" she said to herself.

Yakob had exhausted all the attractions of the many expeditions to be made with Zermatt as a centre, and as a last resort, to furnish an excuse for not attempting the grand ascension, he feigned a sprained ankle. The Judge accepted the situation. It was manifestly impossible for Yakob to guide him up the Matterhorn until he should recover. Meantime, with commendable patience, he contented himself with tending the cows with Annette, Nikolas, and the great dog. The summer had advanced, and they had cropped all the pasturage in the vicinity of the Alm. It was necessary to drive them every morning far up the mountain, to a nook from which the snow had but lately melted, and the grass had a spring-like juiciness. They would set out after the morning milking, carrying their luncheon with them, and would not return until evening. One morning, after they were well on their way, a spirit of perverseness seemed to enter into Brown Velvet, and she deviated from the regular route, plunging down a path which led to the Matterhorn glacier. It was all that Annette could do, by placing herself directly in the way, and striking lusty blows, to keep the other cows from following their leader. She was effectually aided by the dog, and succeeded at last in getting the herd started upon the right path.

"Take them on to the pasture," said the Judge, "and Nikolas and I will go after Brown Velvet. We will soon find her and rejoin you."

Nikolas had greatly improved under Margaret's tuition. He was not really wanting, but simply very backward in expressing the intelligence which he really possessed, and his deformed figure so greatly shocked strangers that he gloated in the terror and disgust which he excited, and, up to Margaret's coming, had made no attempt to contradict the general impression that he was a hopeless cretin, with only a capacity for malice. Margaret was the first outside his immediate family who had overcome her first repugnance, and had treated him kindly. She believed in his capacity and encouraged him to show it. The Judge, too, took a marked interest in him, and he began to pick up English words with a rapidity really remarkable. As they hurried down the mountain together, following Brown Velvet, Nikolas capered on in advance with great glee. He had heard Katchen's legend of the fairy cows, and had understood more of it than any one suspected; for when they reached the glacier and found that Brown Velvet had disappeared from view, he spread out his arms to mimic the action of flying and pointed to the Matterhorn.

The Judge understood him. "You think Brown Velvet has gone to the enchanted pastures on the top of the mountain?"

Nikolas nodded energetically, and ran on all the more eagerly, beckoning and calling, "Come, come! Claus know short way."

"Do you really know the way to the top of the Matterhorn?"

Nikolas nodded again, very knowingly. "Claus been there," he said.

It was possible, the Judge thought, for the dwarf was stronger than most men, and could run and leap and skip over the most dangerous cliffs, and face without dizziness the deepest precipices. He had more than once failed to come back at nightfall from his long rambles, and could not or would not give an account of where he had been. The Judge suspected that Yakob had no intention of guiding him up the Matterhorn, and here was a most tempting opportunity. The way was plain enough; it seemed impossible to miss it; it was still early in the morning. They were provided with luncheon, with alpenstocks, matches, a pocket telescope, and compass. What a fine idea it would be to escape this rather vexatious surveillance and surprise them all by making the ascent! He had no faith in the pretty fancy of the fairy cows, but he was willing to humor Nikolas's belief in it in order to secure his companionship. He accordingly took out his telescope and pretended to be anxiously scanning the sides of the Matterhorn in search of Brown Velvet. At the edge of the glacier they met a peasant boy, and the Judge, with consideration for Margaret's anxiety, wrote her a note telling her of his determination, and that she must not be alarmed if he did not return on the next day. "If you can send some one with a good supper to meet us at the half-way cabin on our return to-morrow evening," he concluded, "it would be a noble idea. I have just bought a bottle of milk and a hare of this peasant, which will provision the expedition until then."

The Judge hurried on with the feeling of wicked elation experienced by a naughty school-boy who is playing truant, mingled with a haunting fear that he might be overtaken and dragged back. On receiving the note, the peasant had set out immediately for the Alm; but the Judge recalled him, as this last apprehension occurred to him, and managed to make the boy understand that there was no hurry, and the note need not be delivered until toward evening.

They proceeded across the glacier with so little difficulty that the Judge's confidence in his young guide increased, and he felt sure that he must have been over the ground before. But how wide the glacier was! They had been walking for a long time, and the great icy river was only half crossed. The Judge began to be very hungry, and Nikolas took a hard crust of black bread from his pocket, and gnawed it ravenously. A little farther on, they came to a broken branch of a pine-tree which had been carried by the moving ice from far up the mountain. It was too good an opportunity to be lost; and the Judge cut up the branch with his great jack-knife, and soon kindled a little fire. "This is something like, at last," he said to Nikolas, as he delightedly warmed his hands over the blaze. "Now, if we only had some coffee! However, we can heat the milk, and we can roast the hare." They enjoyed their picnic keenly, eating only a part of the hare, and wrapping up the remainder for their breakfast. After the meal they proceeded on their way, crossing the remainder of the glacier in a short time, and striking up a long couloir or gully between the slopes on the other side. It was shaded by high cliffs, and paved with smooth, hard snow, easy to walk upon. The Judge could not see the cabin; but he doubted not that this was the regular way, and that a sudden turn would bring them to it. He trudged on

THE REAL THING AT LAST.

gleefully, and, ignorant of the danger which he incurred, began to sing "Marching through Georgia." The cliffs echoed the strains resoundingly, until it almost seemed as if a small portion of Sherman's army was tramping up the white road. Suddenly there was a report like that of a pistol; then the Judge felt the sheet of snow on which he stood sliding under him, slowly at first, but with increasing rapidity. Nikolas shrieked aloud, "An avalanche!"

Swifter and swifter, like the rush of a toboggan, the cake of snow on which they stood sped onward. Paralyzed with terror, they watched the front edge of this cake crumbling and breaking into fine spray as they drove onward. Would the cake last until they reached the glacier at the foot of the couloir? the Judge wondered, when suddenly a new danger loomed ahead. Right before them, the couloir was divided by a crag: one branch — the one up which they had come — leading down to the glacier; the other, to the right of the rock, descended steeply for a little distance, and then ended at the brink of a precipice, a wide crevasse between the glacier and the side of the mountain. Which way would the snow toboggan take? There was no means of guiding it, — and the moment of suspense which ensued was terrible. To the Judge's horror, the cake of snow struck the crag fairly in the centre, and was broken into a hundred pieces. Buried under the loose snow and by the following mass, he was still rolled on, in which direction he could not tell. Then there was a sense of suffocation, a fall, and he knew no more.

CHAPTER X.

LOST!

Here let us leave him — for his shroud the snow;
   For funeral lamps he has the planets seven;
For a great sign the icy stair shall go
   Between the heights to heaven.

One moment stood he as the angels stand,
   High in the stainless eminence of air;
The next he was not, to his fatherland
   'Translated unaware.
                   MYERS.

THE Judge was only too successful in his escapade. Annette remained all day with the cattle at the upper pasture. She was not alarmed that the Judge and Nikolas did not rejoin her; for she presumed that they had been wearied by their chase after Brown Velvet and had decided to remain with her at the Alm. The peasant did not need the Judge's parting admonition to take his own time; for he was on his way to a distant châlet and had decided that he could most conveniently deliver the note to Margaret on his return that evening.

In happy unconsciousness of her grandfather's danger, Margaret passed a delightful day. She was relieved from the cheese-making by Yakob, who ceased limping as soon as the Judge was out of sight, and, taking a bit of embroidery and some of her grandfather's books, she wandered with Katchen to her favorite nook, the shelf of rock which commanded the grand view of the Matterhorn, the spot where she had paused on her way to the Alm two months before, and had bidden farewell to the old life of frivolity and accepted the unknown new life.

She smiled at the trepidation and stern resolve with which she had approached the change. It all seemed so simple and sweet to her now. These poor people had received her so kindly and had taken her to their hearts so cordially that she loved them all. She could see, too, that she was doing them all good. Even Annette, though she was still inexplicable in her varying moods, was sometimes wonderfully devoted, rising early and doing all that she could for Margaret before it was time to drive the cows to pasture. Just how it was all to end she was not sure. Her parents had written inviting the Lochwalders to remove to America, but the old mother and Yakob were not willing to emigrate. They were contented as they were and too old, they said, to learn new ways. Yakob had given her the children, and Margaret pleased herself with thinking how pretty Katchen would change and improve with American influences and education. Of Nikolas's musical ability she had high hopes. He was so fond of her, too, and would rub his shaggy head against her dress in such an affectionate, doggish way, evidently striving to express by actions the love which he could not tell in words. Annette, under her unloving exterior, was passionately attached to her unfortunate cousin. At first his attachment to Margaret filled her with angry jealousy; but as she could not help seeing how patiently Margaret strove to release his poor imprisoned mind, she experienced a vague remorse for her own unworthy deception. Her revenge was not bringing her the satisfaction which she anticipated, but her pride and obstinacy kept her from confessing her fraud.

As Margaret sat that morning on the brink of the precipice, she thought of Wordsworth's lines, —

> Beneath these mountains many a soft vale lies,
> And lofty springs give birth to lowly streams.

Life, even here, was not so stern and savage as it had seemed at first. She had wished to know the real life of the poor. She had shared their experiences, and had found humble pleasures mingled with the toil; for love sweetens all things. She was sure now that true friendship was better than rank or wealth. And she was thankful that so many friendships had come into her life. There was one friend whom she counted true, but from whom she had not heard for several months. Where among these mountain paths and glaciers was Livingston Walker? She had thought of him that morning when the music-box played the air of Cecilia's song, —

> The winter may perish, the spring pass away,
> The summer may fade, and the year decay,
> Thou wilt be mine, thou wilt return to me :
> I've promised to wait, and I'll truly wait for thee.
>
> God help thee if still the sun shines on thee,
> God bless thee if before his glory thou be ;
> I'll wait for thee, and I'll not wait in vain ;
> For if thou wait'st above, ah ! then we'll meet again.

It was a lame translation, and she had scoffed at the sentiment; but there was something in it which touched her now, and tears, for which she could have given no reason, sprang to her eyes. She brushed them away quickly; for some one below the cliff was singing that very song. Some one was coming up the mountain-path. An elastic, eager footstep measured the rocky way with long strides, and sent the pebbles rolling down the cliff. She knew who it was before she looked up. Livingston Walker had come at last. It lacked only this to make the day a perfect one, and she greeted him with more of pleasure than surprise. "This is even finer than the Wengern Alp, is it not?" she said; and the young man acknowledged that it was. He had come from the Grimsel on foot by way of Visp and the St. Nicholas Valley; and he had much to tell her of his adventures since he had last seen her on the glacier of the Aar and on the Great Aletsch Glacier, as well as of a trip through the Austrian Tyrol.

"It seems very natural to see you again," said Margaret; "but how did you know that we were here?"

"I received a letter from your grandfather a week since, telling me of your wanderings, and inviting me to come and ascend the Matterhorn with him."

"You don't mean to encourage him in that insane idea?"

"On the contrary, I thought that I might be of use about this time in suggesting something a little more feasible,— Mont Blanc, for instance. I would like to make that ascent myself before I return to America. From his letter I judged that your grandfather was getting restless. He says, 'They watch me as if I were a child, and throw all manner of obstacles in the way of my attemping the Matterhorn; but some fine day I shall give them the slip.'"

"You are just in time," Margaret replied. "I was wishing only yesterday that you were here. I think grandfather ought to go away from this vicinity for a time. The Matterhorn exercises such a fascination over him. I do not wonder, it is so defiantly beautiful. Look, Mr. Walker! Did you ever see anything more magnificent?"

"It does indeed remind me of our day on the Wengern Alp," Walker replied. "Did you notice that avalanche? We are too far away to hear the reverberations, but the puff of snow-spray was plainly discernible."

"I was just reading about an avalanche," Margaret replied. "Perhaps you would like to continue the reading while I embroider."

Mr. Walker examined the book. "It is the account of the death of the guide Bennen, one of the best descriptions of an avalanche ever written. I will read it with pleasure:—

* "'On Feb. 28, 1864, we (M. Gossett and M. Boissonnet) left Sion with Bennen to mount the Haut de Cry. We started at 2.15 A.M., in a light carriage, that brought us to the village of Ardon, distant six miles. We there met three men that were to accompany us as local guides. . . . We had to go up a steep snow-field about eight hundred

feet high. It was about one hundred and fifty feet broad at the top, and four hundred or five hundred at the bottom. Bennen did not seem to like the look of the snow. He asked the guides whether avalanches ever came down this couloir, to which they answered that our position was perfectly safe. Having arrived at one hundred and fifty feet from the top we began crossing. At about three-quarters of the breadth of the couloir the two leading men sank considerably above their waists. The snow was too deep to think of getting out of the hole they had made, so they advanced, dividing the snow with their bodies. This furrow was about twelve feet long, and, as the snow was good on the other side, we had all come to the false conclusion that the snow was accidentally softer there than elsewhere. Boissonnet advanced, and we heard a deep, cutting sound. The snow-field split in two about fourteen or fifteen feet above us. The cleft was at first quite narrow, not more than an inch broad. An awful silence ensued. It lasted but a few seconds, and then it was broken by Bennen's voice, "Wir sind alle verloren." His words were slow and solemn; they were his last. I drove my alpenstock into the snow, and brought the weight of my body to bear on it; it went in to within three inches of the top. I then waited. It was an awful moment of suspense. I turned my head towards Bennen to see whether he had done the same thing. To my astonishment I saw him turn round, face the valley, and stretch out both arms. The ground on which we stood began to move slowly, and I felt the uselessness of my alpenstock. I soon sank up to my shoulders. The speed of the avalanche increased rapidly, and before long I was covered up with snow, and in utter darkness. I was suffocating, when with a jerk I suddenly came to the surface again. The rope had caught. I was on a wave of the avalanche, and saw it before me. It was the most awful sight I ever witnessed. The head of the avalanche was preceded by a thick cloud of snow-dust, the rest of the avalanche was clear. Around me I heard the horrid hissing of the snow, and far

THE GREAT ALETSCH GLACIER.

before me the thundering of the foremost part of the avalanche. To prevent myself sinking again, I made use of my arms, much in the same way as when swimming in a standing position. At last I noticed that I was moving slower; then I saw the pieces of snow in front of me stop at some yards distance; then the snow straight before me stopped, and I heard on a large scale the same creaking sound that is produced when a heavy cart passes over hard, frozen snow in winter. I felt that I also had stopped, and instantly threw up both arms, to protect my head in case I should again be covered up. I had stopped, but the snow behind me was still in motion. Its pressure on my body was so strong that I thought I should be crushed to death. This pressure ceased as suddenly as it had begun. I was then covered up by snow coming from behind me. My first impulse was to try to uncover my head, but this I could not do. The avalanche had frozen by pressure the moment it stopped, and I was frozen in. Whilst trying vainly to move my arms I became aware that the hands as far as the wrist had the faculty of motion. The conclusion was easy — they must be above the snow. I set to work. At last I saw a faint glimmer of light. The crust above my head was getting thinner, but I could not reach it any more with my hands. The idea struck me that I might pierce it with my breath. After several efforts I succeeded, and felt suddenly a rush of air toward my mouth. After a few minutes I heard a man shouting. What a relief it was to know that I was not the sole survivor: three others were alive. I was at length taken out. The snow had to be cut with the axe down to my feet before I could be pulled out. When I was taken out of the snow the cord had to be cut. We tried the end going toward Bennen, but could not move it. It went nearly straight down, and showed us that there was the grave of the bravest guide the Valais ever had. The cold had done its work; we could stand it no longer, and began the descent. In five hours we reached Ardon.'"

"How shocking to leave the poor man in that way!" Margaret exclaimed.

"It was impossible for them to do otherwise," Mr. Walker replied, "and even if they could have exhumed him at once, they would have found only his lifeless body."

"What folly mountaineering is!" Margaret exclaimed. "No one has a right to risk life unless for the sake of saving life."

As she spoke, Katchen came toward them. "Grandmother has come back from Zermatt, and dinner is ready. I told her there was company and I have cooked some sausages and cabbage."

"What a pretty child!" said Mr. Walker.

"This is my little cousin Katchen," Margaret replied. "Did not grandfather tell you that we had found my relations? They are very worthy people, and I am very fond and proud of them."

MOTHER LOCHWALDER.

To say that Mr. Walker was not surprised to find that Margaret was connected with such lowly peasants, would be untrue. He shook hands, however, with Mother Lochwalder — who congratulated herself that she had on her best clothes — and with Yakob — in his poorest — with a simple friendliness which had nothing in it of condescension, and accepted, with evident pleasure, the invitation to remain and share the Judge's loft, until they should set out upon their expedition to Mont Blanc. Down in his heart of hearts he was very happy. He loved Margaret, but had feared that this love would bring him only grief, for hitherto he had not dared to hope. It seemed to him that with all her grand qualities she was haughty and unapproachable. He saw her now in another character, stooping so sweetly to these humble people, and he said to himself, "She has come to understand real values; when she decides it will be from the highest motives."

Annette returned a little later than usual that afternoon; for she lacked Brown Velvet's assistance in marshalling the herd. She was surprised at not finding the pet cow in her stall, and Yakob was equally astonished at not hearing her bell as the cattle came down the mountain. "Have not Judge Houghton and Nikolas returned?" Annette asked.

"Surely not. Have they not been with you all the day?"

There was great alarm in the châlet when Annette explained how the Judge and Nikolas had gone in search of Brown Velvet, early in the morning.

"The fairy cow has led them straight to the Matterhorn," said Mother Lochwalder.

"It needed no elfin spell to do that," said Margaret; and their worst fears were realized when a little later the peasant arrived, bearing the Judge's cheerful missive.

"We must organize a search-party at once," said Mr. Walker.

"We shall have moonlight, and we can overtake them before morning at the cabin," said Yakob, "if we set out at once. You and I will be enough to bring them back safely: let us waste no time in getting men from Zermatt; we know well enough where they have gone."

He took down a coil of rope and a small pickaxe, while Mother Lochwalder filled a flask with Kirchenwasser and trimmed a lantern. "Hang this outside the cabin if you find them," she said. "We will take the spyglass and watch from the cliff."

Mr. Walker ran back after he had started. Margaret hurried to meet him, thinking that he had forgotten something. He took her hand, and said earnestly, "When I bring your grandfather back safe, Miss Margaret, I shall have a request to make of you. Can you give me the hope that you will grant it?"

"Yes, yes. Of course — anything," Margaret replied, not comprehending him. "But hurry. And Nikolas. Remember, you must bring Nikolas too." The girl's heart sank as she saw them go; and she called back the old peasant who was setting out for Zermatt, and sent a note by him to one of the best guides in the town, asking him to get together a party of the most intrepid mountaineers to follow Mr. Walker and Yakob. Then there was nothing to do but to wait — the hardest task of all. The sun was setting, when, from their post of observation, the women saw the two men begin to cross the glacier. They had found the Judge's trail, and followed it with happy confidence. The moon had risen before the setting of the sun, and with the aid of the glass, the three women saw their friends cross the great white highway, — only two little black specks moving so painfully and slowly, as it seemed to the eager watchers, though they were really making very good time.

It will be remembered that the cake of snow, which carried the Judge and Nikolas down the couloir, split in two against a pinnacle of rock, and that one half swept downward to the glacier, while the other carried the unfortunate mountaineers down a branch couloir into a crevasse at some distance from the point at which they began their ascent. Before Mr. Walker and Yakob had finished crossing the glacier, they saw plainly enough that a recent avalanche had descended the very couloir to which the track they were following led. Fresh snow obliterated the footprints, and the Judge's alpenstock, which had been whirled from his hand by striking against the pinnacle, and had followed the course of this part of the snow-slide, lay at a little distance. The conclusion was most natural that the Judge himself and his little guide were buried under that mass of snow. Yakob began to dig wildly near the spot where he had found the alpenstock. Walker strode up and down, carefully examining the snow for other indications, and hallooing at intervals.

RESCUING PARTY ON THE MATTERHORN.

Margaret saw the pause at the foot of the couloir, and the wavering motion of the lantern as Mr. Walker carried it from one side of the avalanche to the other, and immediately surmised that they had come upon some casualty. At the same time, Annette uttered an exclamation, and pointed to a line of men connected by a rope like so many beads on a rosary, crossing the glacier lower down. "It is the rescuing party from Zermatt," she said; "but they do not see father and Mr. Walker, and are going to begin the ascent of the mountain at another point, and will be of no help."

"If we could only attract their attention by signals of some sort," Margaret suggested, "and make them understand that they are needed in the other direction."

They lighted torches of pine fagots, and waved them frantically; but with no effect. The human rosary wound around the base of the mountain, and was lost to view. Mother Lochwalder groaned, and wrung her hands.

"Perhaps grandfather and Nikolas have really succeeded in reaching the cabin," Margaret suggested; "and it is all for the best that the men have gone that way."

ON THE MATTERHORN.

"No, no!" replied Mother Lochwalder. "Yakob would never stop where he is now if some dreadful accident had not happened."

"It is all my fault," Margaret said penitently. "If I had only allowed Cousin Yakob to go with grandfather, he would have brought him back safely."

"Praise be to the Virgin, that he did not go with him," Mother Lochwalder replied. "If your grandfather had been lost under Yakob's guidance, our family would have been cursed indeed. It is just what I have been dreading ever since you came,—the punishment of the crime of one of your ancestors visited upon another. I knew the Matterhorn would have justice done, and I have sometimes feared that Yakob might have to pay the debt. Better so, than that two innocent ones should perish. But I am thankful that it cannot be said that he was the means of their destruction."

"What do you mean, aunt?" Margaret asked, entirely unable to comprehend her meaning.

"She is wild," Annette replied. "The anxiety of this night has crazed her. Pay no attention to what she says, she has lost her wits."

"You speak lies, granddaughter," replied the old woman shortly. "My lady grand-niece has asked to know the reason why my brother left his native land, and lived under an assumed name in a distant country. I will not conceal it from her any longer. Know, my child, that your Grandfather Lochwalder was one of the best guides in the country; but one woful day he guided a wealthy man up the Matterhorn."

"Well?"

"No; it was not well. The man was not experienced in mountaineering. He slipped, and was dashed in pieces on the rocks a thousand feet below."

"Horrible!" Margaret replied. "Poor grandfather how he must have suffered!"

"Yes; poor man, poor man! Better have lain in the place of the traveller, dead, in the deep ravine, for the finger of scorn was pointed at him by every hand in the valley; and his old friends turned the cold shoulder, and would not recognize him."

"Why, I think they ought to have sympathized with him in his great misfortune."

"They said that they were tied together; and if the rope had held, the stranger would have been safe; for my brother was strong and able to brace himself like an ox, and the stranger slender and of light weight."

"But if the rope broke, it surely was not grandfather's fault."

"The rope did not break. They who found the body brought it to the Commune. The rope was cut clean in two by the sharp blade of a hunting-knife. They said that my brother had led the man to a dangerous spot; and when he was pulling on the rope to help himself up the slippery way, the scoundrel with one gash had cut the cord, and let him fall to his death, meaning to find and rob the body afterward."

"But it was a lie, aunt; they were all liars. Cousin Yakob said my grandfather was an honest man. It is impossible that my grandfather could have committed such a crime. He may have been poor, but he could not have been wicked."

Annette laughed a cruel, bitter laugh. "Why not your grandfather, as well as another? Do you think that you are not also human? Now you know something of the troubles of the poor. It is not hunger of body or mind which is hardest to bear, but shame for evil deeds of our own and of those we love — deeds to which you rich are never tempted. My great-uncle did not deliberately commit murder for the sake of gold. The man had fallen over the side of the precipice. The rock on which the guide stood was slippery; with one hand he had grasped a bush, and he felt to his horror that it was giving way. It was not possible for him to brace himself, for his feet could gain no hold on the icy rock. It was a question whether one man or two men should perish. He had but an instant to decide; and — he confessed it to his sister — he did cut the rope."

Margaret uttered a low cry. "The coward! he should have died first!"

"It is easy to say that," Mother Lochwalder replied. "The poor boy realized it himself afterward. But what can we do when our friends choose wrongly? Only forgive them, and love them, and try to help them bear their shame with them as best you can. When I saw my brother grovelling on the floor before me and asking me to kill him, I said, 'Brother, we must not commit two crimes. Go to a new country and live a new life, and God will know what is best for you here and hereafter.' He wound the rope which he had cut about his body under his shirt. 'I shall wear it till my death,' he said, 'to keep me from forgetting my crime.' I packed a sack with his clothes, and he set out by way of the Theodule Pass; but the townspeople were watching all the roads, and they were posted there, too, and they dragged him back to jail. He knew that he would be tried for murder and hung, and he could not bear it. The window of his cell overlooked a ravine; and one dark night he removed a bar and fastened one end of the rope to the grating. Then he squeezed through the upper part of the window and descended the rope hand over hand. When he had reached the end he was still many feet above the ground. He was afraid to let go, and might have swung there until he was caught,— for you say right, he was a coward,— but the rope which had held the poor traveller on the Matterhorn broke under my brother's weight, and he fell to the ground, bruised, but not badly injured. The Theodule Pass was not guarded that night; for they thought him safe in prison. I never saw him again, or heard from him or his until Annette, who went away to America long after, wrote me that she had found you."

The story was told, and Margaret wound her arms around Mother Lochwalder. "You were right, dear aunt," she said. "All we can do is to love the erring, forgive and help them, and bear the consequences of their sin. I accept this legacy also, and I will try to help you bear your trouble."

Annette looked at Margaret in a dazed way. She could not believe her ears. "Such goodness is not human," she thought. "It is only the stress of this intense excitement which has brought out such a theatrical declaration. To-morrow, when her grandfather is found, she will shake us all off and leave us."

Mother Lochwalder was wearied with watching and emotion, and Margaret led her gently inside the châlet and persuaded her to lie down. Mother Lochwalder urged Margaret to follow her example.

"You will make yourself ill, and be of no service when they come back," she argued. "You are as white as a ghost now."

"I am cramped with sitting still; I am wild from doing nothing," Margaret replied. "I am going down to the glacier."

"You cannot see as much there as here."

But Margaret did not hear her. She could bear the inaction no longer, and had hurried down the mountain-side. Annette followed, telling herself fiercely that Margaret's anxiety was all for her grandfather, and that she cared nothing for the poor lost child.

The Zermatt glacier is impressive even in daylight. Ruskin has best described it in this inimitable word-picture: "Higher up the ice opens into broad white fields and furrows, hard and dry, scarcely fissured at all except just under the Cervin, and forming a silent and solemn causeway, paved, as it seems, with white marble from side to side: broad enough for the march of an army in line of battle, but quiet as a street of tombs in a buried city, and bordered on each hand by ghostly cliffs of that faint granite purple which seems, in its far-away height, as unsubstantial as the dark blue that bounds it; the whole scene so changeless and soundless, so removed, not merely from the presence of men, but even from their thoughts, so destitute of all life of tree or herb, and so immeasurable in its lonely brightness of majestic death, that it looks like a world from which not only the human, but the spiritual, presences had perished, and the last of its archangels, building the great mountains for their monuments, had laid themselves down in the sunlight to an eternal rest, each in his white shroud."

As Margaret stood upon the edge of the glacier in the ghostly moonlight, she was almost overpowered by its awful loneliness and sublimity. She walked a little way forward, and then a great trembling seized her and she stood still. She had lost one grandfather this night. Her ideal, chivalric grandfather, who had left Europe an exile for the sake of his conviction, was no more. In his place she must accept the memory of a fugitive criminal. And her own loved Grandfather Houghton, with the boyish heart,— where was he? Suddenly, far off across the snow-field, she saw Mr. Walker and Yakob, and oh, joy! between them they supported the dear old man, rescued from a living grave. After the first wild thrill of joy she looked again for Nikolas. He was so tiny she might well have missed him. Surely he was following behind the rest. Annette overtook her, and she begged her anxiously to look. "You can see better than I, Annette. Where is Nikolas?"

"He is not with them. He must be lost."

The three came on, with white, sad faces.

"Nikolas!" cried Margaret, "where is Nikolas?" The tears were streaming down the Judge's face; he could not reply, and Yakob answered solemnly, "It is the revenge of the Matterhorn. A stranger was killed that one of our family might live, and now Nikolas pays the debt. God's will be done."

"Oh, no, no!" Margaret exclaimed. "It is not the will of our Father in Heaven that one of these little ones should perish! You found my grandfather. Why did you not dig further and find Cousin Nikolas?"

"Our strength is exhausted," Mr. Walker replied. "We could do no more."

"The other party has gone up the mountain; I will go after them!" Margaret exclaimed.

"You are crazy!" Annette exclaimed. "Do you not see that your grandfather is nearly fainting, and the others are worn out? Between us, we will get him to the châlet. What matters it if a poor deformed dwarf is lost?"

"My dear cousin, you can help grandfather. I will go to Zermatt and get together more men, and show them where to go."

Mr. Walker called to her, "Come back; it is of no use!" but they could not stop her, she was running down the path that skirted the glacier. The moon had set and the dawn was breaking gray and chill, and she looked like a phantom of the mists. "God bless her," said Yakob reverently, "how she loves the boy!"

And Annette, winding her strong arm about the Judge, as she supported him up the path toward the châlet, felt all the bitter waters of hatred toward Margaret ebb from her heart, and a great surging wave of love roll in. "Is there any hope?" she asked of Mr. Walker and Yakob, who were tottering after her.

"We found the Judge in a shallow crevasse, only partially buried," replied the younger man, "and we went over the entire avalanche, thrusting our alpenstocks deep into the snow at near intervals. Nothing living could exist below that depth."

"No," added Yakob, with a sob. "My boy is dead, — but God bless her all the same!"

CHAPTER XI.

THE WAGNER FESTIVAL. BAVARIA.

MRS. NEWTON, Alice, and Cecilia, after the departure of the others for the south, turned their steps toward the northeast.

By making a slight detour from the direct route to Zurich, they could visit the celebrated abbey church of Einsiedeln; and though it was not yet time for the great annual pilgrimage, when a hundred and fifty to two hundred thousand pilgrims from all parts of Europe visit the spot, they determined to take it on their way.

The abbey is built on the summit of Mt. Etzel, in a wild, desolate region near Lake Zurich.

Tradition states that Meinrad, a noble of the family of Hohenzollern, about one thousand years ago, felt called upon to withdraw from the world, and devote himself to the care of an image of the Virgin given him by Saint Hildegarde, Abbess of Zurich. In 803 he was murdered, but two pet ravens pursued the murderers to Zurich and caused their arrest. They were executed on a spot where now stands the Raven Inn.

The three friends stopped at this inn, and after very simple refreshment, mounted to the great monastery which now occupies the site of Saint Meinrad's cell.

Erberard, another count of the same family, founded this convent here in 948, the emperor granting lands. The Bishop of Constance was to consecrate the church, but was awakened by angelic minstrelsy and the confirmation that the ceremony had already been performed by the Saviour.

Pope Leo VIII. pronounced it a true miracle, and granted indulgence to all pilgrims who should visit the abbey. The spring from which the holy hermit drank has been so conducted into a system of water-works, and gushes from fourteen different pipes in front of the church. The pilgrims feel it necessary to drink from each of these pipes, a hydropathic treatment which may be beneficial for certain disorders. Within the church they were shown the Virgin of Saint Meinrad, an ugly doll of black wood, resembling the devotional images so common in Spain. It was dressed gorgeously in gold brocade and jewels, and the walls of the church were hung with votive offerings from penitents and pilgrims. There were crutches left by the lame who fancied that they had been healed, wax figures of deformities, for which deliverance had been sought, and rich gifts of gold and silver from those who asked plenary indulgence, not only for past, but for contemplated crimes. The pope's remission of sins is inscribed in letters of gold over the door of the church, " Hic est plena remissio pecatorum a poena et a culpa," and many a guilty soul still seeks this shrine to roll away its weight of sin.

The reformer, Zwingli, began his preaching here, and boldly declared at this centre of idolatry, "Christ *alone* saves, and he saves *everywhere*. Do not imagine that God is in this temple more than in any part of creation. Whatever be the country in which you dwell, God is around you and hears you."

As the girls were shown the beautiful objects of the goldsmith's art, left as votive offerings, Cecilia uttered an exclamation of surprise. "Only look at this, Alice," and she pointed to a silver vinaigrette, "it is undoubtedly the one which the countess lost; see, it bears the engraved crest, a mailed hand holding a firebrand."

Mrs. Newton asked the sacristan who had given the object; but the man could only tell that it had been donated during the previous week, by an unknown woman who had confessed to the priest in charge.

ABBEY OF EINSIEDELN.

"It was undoubtedly Annette," said Cecilia. "But I am astonished; for Margaret assured me that, during her long stay with her mother, the girl has always been strictly honest. Annette never could do the simplest thing without the greatest secrecy. I have fancied for some time that she had something on her conscience which is troubling her. Doubtless, she has been here at Einsiedeln to seek absolution for this first theft, and is now on her way to her people. But what could have induced her to steal the thing?" Cecilia questioned, much puzzled. It was impossible to induce the guardians of the church property to give up the vinaigrette on their testimony; and the travellers continued their journey, without being able to arrive at an explanation of the mystery.

They had left Switzerland, and with only a brief stop at Stuttgart and Nuremberg, proceeded to Baireuth, where they had planned to spend several weeks in the enjoyment of the Wagner Festival. It was not the regular year for it; but fortunately for them, the Emperor of Germany had requested a special performance of the operas, and they, with many other tourists, would benefit by the request.

The friends reached Baireuth, a small town in Northern Bavaria, in the latter part of July. The sleepy old town seems surprised by the sudden notoriety forced upon it by the festivals which are held here in honor of Wagner. Hundreds of visitors from every part of the world are attracted by the musical treat. No adequate accommodations are provided for them; and the townspeople incommode themselves, and huddle into corners, without furnishing the necessary room for their guests.

The girls walked from house to house, and at last were obliged to content themselves with very inconvenient quarters. If the rooms were undesirable, they had the merit of cheapness. Frau Selig, the honest hostess, had no idea of taking advantage of the demand for lodgings by charging an extortionate price. American enterprise, in such a place, would build palatial hotels, and would make a high percentage on the money invested.

The concerts had been in progress for two weeks, and would last a month longer. They were held in a theatre built for the purpose, on a hill about a mile from the town. A performance was given three times a week. The opera of " Parsifal," being the favorite, was given every week, while the programme for the other days was changed frequently.

The opera played the first afternoon after the arrival of the three friends was " The Meistersinger." Taking their landlady's pretty daughter, Minna, with them, they drove out through the shady avenue in the early afternoon, enjoying the beautiful view from the summit of the hill. The performance began at four in the afternoon, and continued for one hour, when there was an intermission of an hour, during which the audience strolled in the woods at the back of the theatre, or patronized the café, returning for the second act; after which another hour of intermission occurred, followed by the third and last act, the concert ending at about nine o'clock.

The girls were struck, on entering the theatre, by one marked peculiarity. There were no lights, and the auditorium was quite dark. This was Wagner's desire, in order that the attention of the audience might not be distracted from the music by familiar faces, or by magnificent costumes. No one attends these operas to see or to be seen, but simply and solely for the sake of the music.

FRAU SELIG.

For a similar reason the orchestra is sunk below the stage, that the dark figures of the musicians may not silhouette against the footlights, and the attention be drawn by the fine bowing of a violinist, or the energetic movements of the conductor's baton.

They were early, and in spite of the dusk, Minna pointed out the different boxes opposite the stage.

MINNA.

"Those are the Starr sisters," said Minna, indicating two old ladies. "They were friends of Wagner, and have not missed a single performance since the festival was instituted. That is his son Siegfried Wagner, who is speaking with them. The central box belongs to Frau Cosima. See! the gracious lady is taking her seat."

"Who is Frau Cosima?" asked Mrs. Newton.

"Who but the widow of the great Wagner, and the daughter of Liszt?"

"Then why is she not called Frau Wagner?"

"It is her Christian name; we call her so in loving familiarity, just as if I were to call you by your Christian name, Lady Alice. She is *the* lady of this region; she was always Cosima to her husband and her father, and she will always be Cosima to us. The other boxes are occupied by royal personages, and by distinguished musical artists. Those seats cannot be had for mere money. Hush, the orchestra are beginning!"

All listened with rapt attention, while the most famous singers of Germany presented even the most subordinate parts.

During the intermission they wandered through the grove, and were surprised to find that the greater part of the audience ignored the café, and seemed in haste to seek the most solitary by-paths. "You thought that Germans cared only for good things to eat, did you not?" asked Minna. "Ah, no! we are the most sentimental people in the world. Why is that tall man taking such long strides over the rocks? It is that he may get away from the crowd and sit down by himself and meditate."

The girls sympathized with the sentimentalist during the first intermission, but at the second recess, the claims of hunger could not be disregarded, and they sustained their higher natures by a visit to the café and a liberal re-inforcement of pretzils and coffee.

The charm of Baireuth grew upon Cecilia, as she lingered under its influence; but Alice said one morning: —

"I am beginning to tire even of our delightful tour; I long to get to my real work among my dear Bulgarian girls."

There were tears in her kindly eyes which were not those of self-pity; for Alice had become interested in Lajos for his own sake. What he had told her of the poor miners had made her feel that he was not altogether selfish. He had said that he wished her to visit his estates, and tell him how he could improve the condition of his tenants; but she had heard nothing from him since they had left Lucerne. The conclusion was natural that he did not care for her, and that his philan-

A DEVOTEE OF WAGNER.

thropic impulse was only a momentary one, or that he was entirely bound by his aunt's whims. With this feeling, Alice put Lajos resolutely from her thoughts, and forced herself to be interested in the musical festival.

They had been in Baireuth a little over a week before she attended the opera of "Parsifal," which is generally conceded to be Wagner's masterpiece. Alice had been prejudiced against Wagner's music, but with Cecilia at her side to explain, the noble moral purpose of this work opened before her, and she understood the grandeur of conception and the elevation of soul which must have stood behind such a composition.

LISTENING TO "PARSIFAL," NO. 1.

Not only was the poetry itself dignified in form and of high order technically,—and this she had not expected, as Wagner's fame as a musical composer overshadows that which he might have won as an author,—but the old myth of the Holy Grail was ennobled in its elaboration in a manner quite worthy of Tennyson. The plot of "Parsifal" reminded the girls of the "Idyls of the King" and the other Arthurian legends; for curiously enough the same traditions of Arthur's court and his knights of the Table Round exist in Germany, and like the English legends, have a Breton origin. The grail was a chalice of chrysolite which Christ is supposed to have used at his last supper with his disciples. It was the favorite quest

LISTENING TO "PARSIFAL," NO. 2.

of the knights of Arthur's court, but only he whose heart was pure could succeed.

During the intermission between the second and third acts Alice and Cecilia followed the general custom in strolling through the grove at the back of the theatre. This is a favorite resort for people from Baireuth, and is frequented by many who do not attend the operas. Seeing so many persons walking about, the girls, who had not happened to hear the trumpet signal which announced the opening of each act, did not realize the flight of time, and found when they returned to the theatre that the performance had begun. They were not allowed to disturb the audience by passing down the aisle to their seats, and the usher could only find a chair for Cecilia, so that Alice found herself standing alone at the back of the darkened auditorium. Presently a gentleman in the next row became aware that a lady was standing, and politely offered her his seat. Alice demurred, but in the midst of her hesitation found herself placed in the seat with gentle firmness. It was Lajos, beaming with a delight which seemed actually to illuminate his features. "This poor Parsifal has found his grail at last," he said with a joyful earnestness which gave the low-spoken words a double and personal meaning.

He stood behind her throughout the remainder of the act, bending once to take the opera-glass which she handed him, and keeping a firm, steady hold of her hand until the falling of the curtain.

Alice knew from that quiet hand-clasp that all her doubts and fears had been groundless; her knight had been wandering in no palace of Klingsor.

After the close of the performance he led her to his aunt, who had a better seat nearer the front. Having just arrived, Lajos had been obliged to content himself with what he could obtain, and the happy chance had occasioned their meeting. "I would have found you in any case," he said afterward, "if I had found it necessary to search from door to door."

The countess received Alice graciously, and inquired where they were staying. "I shall call on your mother to-morrow," she said, "to make arrangements for our journey down the Danube, which I trust we can make in company."

"There are delightful rides to be made on horseback in the vicinity of Baireuth," said Lajos. "Have you seen the ruined castle of Stein in the Fichtelgebirge? Can we not make up a riding-party for to-morrow? Your mother and my aunt can be driven in an open carriage, and we can be their outriders."

This plan was adopted with acclaim; but on the following morning Cecilia found herself suffering from headache, and could not be induced to accompany the party. It was to be an all-day's excursion, and Frau Selig's stout hand-maidens lifted a well-filled lunch hamper into the carriage. Alice, in a handsome green cloth riding-suit, and Lajos, in an Austrian riding-costume, mounted on spirited but gentle horses, led the way. They picknicked in the pine woods, and crossing a spur of the Ochsenkopf, returned toward evening by another route. It was a charming excursion; but they made no attempt to climb to the "Bake Oven," the hut erected by the German Alpine Club on the summit of the Schneeberg; nor were they greatly interested in the enchanting views of Franconian Switzerland, which opened to them at intervals; nor in the fantastic legends which Richter found in this delightful region; and yet they had much to talk of, and the long ride through the shady forest seemed a very short one.

MRS. NEWTON.

When mother and daughter joined each other in their own room, there were tears in Mrs. Newton's gentle eyes.

"The countess has proposed for your hand for her nephew," she said. "This is no surprise to you, my daughter?"

"Lajos has explained everything," Alice replied. "He did not feel at Lucerne that he was free to ask any one to be his wife. Even now he does not know whether he offers me the hand of a comparatively poor man, or that of the owner of the mines. If a young lady to whom he was betrothed in childhood by his aunt and uncle, and whom he has never seen, is found before the fifth of August, he must either marry her — and this he says he will never do — or give up all his fortune. It is all so strange! Did the countess tell you about it?"

"Yes, my dear; and I assured her that I would be better pleased if Lajos were not wealthy, and your fortunes were more equal."

"But in that case he would not be able to benefit these poor people, for whose welfare he is so much concerned."

"The countess tells me that there is no longer any probability of any claimant appearing," said Mrs. Newton. "Long ago she exchanged a pledge with a dear friend, that the children in whom they were most in-

ON· THE FICHTELGEBIRGE.

terested should marry; but the friend died, and the niece has never been heard from, though search has been made for her in Europe and America. She will probably never appear, and her little fortune will remain in Lajos's care, its income legally at his disposal."

"And as long as it rests in this way he can use the income for the poor miners. It is this that reconciles me to the giving up of my work in Bulgaria. The Board can find some one else to take my place there, but there is no one interested to send a missionary to these poor Magyar miners. Lajos says I can go on with the same work that I have been doing; it will only be a change of scene to people a little more forlorn and forgotten of the world."

"You will have an opportunity to see them soon, for the countess desires us to visit with her. She wished the marriage to take place at her chateau; but it seemed to me better that you should proceed to your mission, and take charge there until some one can be secured to take your place. I think I might take it, Alice, if the Board would accept me. I am not so young as you, but I am vigorous, and can look forward to twenty years more of active service."

"Dear mother, Lajos wishes you to make your home with us."

"Not at first, dear. I shall come to you when I can no longer be useful at the mission; but I shall be happier to feel that I have still my own work in the world; and it will be better for you to grow to understand one another without me. I shall be very near, you know, just over the border, and can go to you, or you can come to me, whenever we need each other."

Mrs. Newton was very firm, and this plan was accordingly agreed upon. It seemed to her wise heart that the countess formed an element of sufficient difficulty in the new household without complicating it by the addition of another outsider. But the whimsical countess seemed to have transferred the affection which she had formerly shown to Margaret to Alice. Any mention of Margaret would bring out a tirade against low-born peasants, and she would assert positively that there had always been something common about Margaret, in spite of her attractive qualities.

"Ze blood will tell," she remarked sententiously. "She have ze sprightliness of foots of a chamois. Zat come from her ancestors, who have been long climbers of ze Alps. When she wear ze peasant costume, did I not say to her, it is more becoming to you as to ze uzzers, you wear it as if you have been use to it for always?"

This was undeniable; but Alice was somewhat astonished by her next assertion, that Margaret's inability to do anything at the time when Alice had saved the countess's life had convinced her that Margaret was only a trifling butterfly, while there was something grandly noble in Alice, which was well worthy of confidence and affection.

"I see many a trial for you in the fickleness of the countess," Mrs. Newton remarked to her daughter.

"There are trials everywhere," Alice replied, "and Lajos, at least, is not fickle." The happy confidence with which she said this told how perfect was her trust. But Lajos had not yet undergone the final test of his affection; at least so said pretty Minna Selig, who, dressed as a Hungarian gypsy, told his fortune in a Dresden tea-cup a few nights before they left Baireuth.

"Beware," she said in sport, "a dark, tall woman who is coming to make trouble between you. She is your Fate, the final test of constancy. If your engagement survive her appearing, all will be well."

There was much merry joking after this dismal fortune, and during their remaining stay every tall, mysterious-looking stranger was laughingly called the Fate; but before the close of the musical festival, Mrs. Newton and Alice, the countess and Lajos, left Baireuth in company to sail down the Danube to the old chateau in the Carpathians.

The betrothal had so filled the minds of both Alice and Cecilia that it was not until the day before she left that it occurred to Alice to mention the vinaigrette which they had seen at Einsiedeln. The countess agreed with them that it was very mysterious.

"I care for zat vinaigrette more especially," she said, "for because it is ze only souvenir I have of my tear friend, Margaret Du Fais. She gave it to me ze day we make our scheme for Lajos and her niece. 'Keep it, my tear,' she say, 'and when you shall see it, you shall sink of zis petrothal.' I have kept it all zese year, and when I lose it I say to myself, It is a sign that my tear friend absolve me from zat promise. I shall see it no longer, zerefore I shall sink no more again to find her niece for Lajos. I am glad ze vinaigrette is in a shrine of sacred objects. It was already sacred wiz me. I could not sink it in ze window of ze pawnproker."

And so they went away, all smiling and happy, not realizing that Lajos's test was all the time steadily approaching. Cecilia lingered in Baireuth. She enjoyed the musical atmosphere of the town, and she intended to remain here until it was time to join Margaret at the Fête of the Vignerons at Vevey. One day, as Cecilia was taking her morning walk, she noticed a tall, angular woman approaching from the railroad station. "If Lajos were here," she thought, "we would all say, 'There is your Fate.'" Something familiar in the figure struck her, and she looked again. It was Annette Stauffer.

CHAPTER XII.

THE FAIRY COW.

AS Margaret sped on through the gathering mists, it seemed to her that she heard, across the glacier, the faint tinkle of a silver bell. Was it Brown Velvet? Very likely; but she had no time to investigate the sound; she reached Zermatt much exhausted.

The most experienced mountaineers had gone up the Matterhorn, but another party of peasants was quickly formed. While they were preparing shovels, picks, and ropes, a thoughtful woman brought Margaret a bowl of hot coffee, and a mule was found on which she rode back with the rescuers. She showed them the trail across the glacier to the avalanche, and then mounted to the châlet, falling into Annette's arms in a dead faint, from utter exhaustion, as she reached the door.

When she came to herself she was lying on Mother Lochwalder's feather-bed, and the noonday sun was shining across the floor. Mr. Walker lay on the hay in the opposite corner sleeping soundly. Yakob sat in an attitude of great dejection beside the table. Mother Lochwalder was stirring something over the fire. She came to the bedside a few moments later with a bowl of soup. "Have they come back?" Margaret asked.

The old woman nodded, her face working frightfully.

It was needless to ask anything further, and Margaret drew the poor, bereaved woman down beside her. After a few moments, she rose and asked for her grandfather.

"He is in bed," said Mother Lochwalder, "and doing well."

Margaret stole up to the loft, but finding the Judge sleeping peacefully did not disturb him. As she came down the ladder, she saw that Yakob Lochwalder stood just outside the door and that he beckoned to her. She walked with him out to her favorite seat.

"Annette asked me to give you this," said Yakob, taking a letter from his pocket.

"Where is Annette?" asked Margaret.

"She has gone away."

"Gone away! where?"

"I don't know. When the men that you got together came back and said there was no hope, Annette went into one of her queer fits, and said that she must go away, but would come back after a while, and she wrote this letter and told me to give it to you. Annette is a strange girl, but she loved her little cousin, and his loss has nearly crazed her. She cannot bear to stay here, I suppose. I can understand the feeling."

"When did she go away?"

"Only an hour ago. She must be in Zermatt now waiting for the diligence to Visp."

Margaret began to tear open the letter, when her eye was caught by the words, "Not to be opened until I am far away." Margaret was too honorable not to regard the request, and her hand slipped downward to place the letter in her pocket.

Instinctively, at the same time her gaze turned toward the glacier. A little lower than the spot where the fateful accident occurred, it seemed to her that she saw a dark speck upon the shining whiteness. As she looked at it more attentively, she was positive that it moved. She dropped the letter and caught Yakob's arm. His eyes were better than hers. "It is a cow," he said; "how could she have crossed the ice-field?" Margaret told him of the sound of the bell which she had heard the night before, and Yakob hurried to the châlet for the telescope. After a long, earnest gaze, he handed the glass to Margaret. "It is Brown Velvet," he said; "I suspected it. Now does it not seem as if she must be a fairy cow? For in the first, how could she have reached the point where she is without wings? and then, why should she want to go there at all unless it is to seek the Paradise on the Matterhorn? All the same, I am going after her; she is too good a cow to lose."

"You are too weary."

"No, I have rested; and I cannot bear sitting still and doing nothing. I cannot even dig my poor boy's grave."

He rose heavily, and went into the châlet for his alpenstock, axe, and rope, and calling the dog, went down the path. Mr. Walker came from the châlet with him, and came toward Margaret.

"Are you rested?" she asked.

"Perfectly," he replied seriously; "but my mind is not at rest. You will remember that I told you that if I brought your grandfather back, I should have something to ask you."

A sudden comprehension of what he meant swept over Margaret.

"Oh, no, not now!" she cried.

"But you promised to listen to me, Margaret."

"If you brought Nikolas, too."

He made a despairing gesture. "And, since that is impossible, I am to go away, and never come back?"

"I did not say that. But this poor family is in such trouble, that it is wicked for us to be happy."

He sprung toward her, with a great light on his face; but she avoided him. "I mean it is wicked for us to think of ourselves now. Yes, I do want you to go away for the present, and, meantime, think of Cecilia's song."

Again he strode toward her; but Margaret was half-way to the châlet, and Mother Lochwalder stood in the door. He could only ask the old woman for his knapsack, and take his leave.

Margaret went to her grandfather; he, too, was awake and well, but much shaken by his experience, and thoroughly cured of his desire to climb the Matterhorn. He descended to the living-room, partook of some supper, and watched Mother Lochwalder and Katchen while they brought the cows in from the main pasture, and performed the evening milking. Margaret set the châlet in order, and came and sat beside her grandfather. They were both thinking of Nikolas. Should they never see the elfish little fellow again, seated among the cattle in the pasture, making his grotesque, whimsical faces, or playing delightedly upon the zither?

Suddenly a sweet, low tone thrilled through the quiet, like the vagrant harmonies which he loved to waken. Margaret looked about her furtively. There was no one in sight, and yet the weird music was very real and near. Was it indeed true that the spirits of Zermatt peasants lingered after death near their old homes, loth to leave the pleasant pastures even for Paradise? A moment's search revealed the source of the strange sounds. It was really the zither, with which Katchen had propped open the window, and the evening breeze was playing upon it as on an æolian harp. Margaret sighed, when she made the discovery. It was sweet to think that Nikolas was near.

He was nearer than she thought. When the cake of snow on which the Judge and Nikolas were carried down the couloir split in two against the rocky buttress, they were carried in different directions, — the Judge, to the glacier, down the path up which they had climbed; and Nikolas, lower down into a ravine in the mountain leading to a crevasse between the mountain and the glacier. The snow beneath him broke his fall. The snow that followed partially buried him; but the boy struggled to the surface, in no way injured by his adventure. He wandered down the long, narrow ravine to the crevasse, whose steep sides were formed on the one hand by a wall of rock, and on the other by one of ice. He walked along it for fully a quarter of a mile, but could find no way of mounting to the surface. If he had had his pick, he could easily have cut steps in the perpendicular wall; but unfortunately he had nothing with which to dig, not even a jack-knife. Night came quickly, and although it was midsummer, the icy wall made the ravine, wide as it was, very cold. To keep off the deadly chill, he spent the entire night walking up and down the ravine. He shouted at intervals, but he was too far away from the rescuers to be heard. How long the night seemed! The moon looked down upon him, and he sang and chattered to her, — scolding her at first, for her indifference to his misfortune, and finally beseeching her to help him. But the moon gave him no help beyond lighting him over the rough places, and giving him a feeling of companionship. Toward morning, even she withdrew; and there were several hours of darkness, which gradually brightened, through murky mists, into a cold, gray dawn. To keep his heart up, in this most dismal part of his experience, he yodelled cheerily to the lady moon, with the childish hope that he might lure her back.

Evidently the moon did not hear him; but there was a friend who caught the faint sound of the distant yodel, and who made her way painfully across the glacier toward him. That friend was Brown Velvet. Margaret heard her bell as she started on her trip, but she did not hear the call which had attracted the faithful animal. When the sun rose, Nikolas, who was slapping his arm across his chest, and stamping his half-frozen feet, heard the musical tinkle of the silver bell, and looking up, saw the cow looking down wistfully at him. The sight revived his sinking courage. He sang and danced, and talked to her most affectionately.

"Good Brown Velvet; dear, beautiful, wise Brown Velvet; unfold your butterfly wings, and float down into the crevasse, and bear me up to the Paradise on the Matterhorn. You see that I am dead and buried, Brown Velvet."

The cow continued to regard him plaintively with her great gazelle-like eyes.

"Ah! I see, then, that I cannot be dead; for it is only dead

NIKOLAS.

people that go to Paradise. Then, Brown Velvet, go back to the Alm, and tell the people to come and fetch me."

The cow lowed as though striving to call the boy's friends, but did not leave him.

"I am hungry, Brown Velvet. I wish you were near enough for me to milk you. Ah! I had forgotten; here is the rest of the hare safe inside my blouse. It will make a good breakfast. I wish I could give you some." Nikolas improvidently devoured his entire provision, and somewhat refreshed, set himself to walking again, the cow following him along the edge of the crevasse. All day long he wandered, fruitlessly striving to extricate himself from his predicament. He managed about noon, with a sharp stone, to cut some steps in the ice, and mounted nearly to the surface, but fell back and twisted his ankle, so that he could walk no longer. He was ready for dinner now, and so was Brown Velvet. She had drunk a little melted snow water, but had begun to think regretfully of the pastures and fodder-rack of the Alm. She turned, and Nikolas heard her bell

A PEASANT OF ZERMATT.

tinkling off into the distance. It seemed to him that he had lost his last friend, and he yodelled loudly. The cow, true to her training, returned, but wandered restlessly about the spot. Nikolas knew that he could not live through another night in the ravine now that he was deprived of the power of keeping himself warm by walking. He wondered, too, how he was to provide himself with dinner or supper, and regretted his greediness of the morning. He remembered one of his father's fabulous hunting stories of how a chamois hunter had fallen into an abyss so deep that it was impossible to find ropes long enough to pull him out; and his true love came every morning and threw provisions down to him, and continued her ministrations until her lover died of old age.

His ankle was swelling, and he wrapped it in snow, and then, dragging himself back into the ravine as far from the glacier as possible, tried to dig a little cave for himself in the mountain side, where the stony wall was crumbling, but soon found that this was useless. Some crows sailed over far up in the blue, and he wished hungrily that he had his father's gun, that he might bring one down for supper. His strength and courage were ebbing fast, and he tried to repeat his little evening prayer, but could only remember the first two lines:

> O, Jesu mein, ganz bin ich dein
> Im Leben und im Sterben.

It seemed to him that he heard his father calling the cows and singing a stanza of the familiar "Ranz des Vaches." It was no dream; for Brown Velvet heard it, too, and frisked away from the brink of the crevasse. He tried to yodel, but the sound died in his throat in a hoarse gurgle, and he lost all consciousness.

Yakob had only come part way across the glacier, and had then sent the dog to drive Brown Velvet to him as he stood calling her. The dog obeyed his bidding, frisking about the cow in wide circles and driving her toward his master. In one of these circles he looked down into the crevasse and spied Nikolas. Instantly the intelligent creature stood still and barked to attract his master's attention. But Yakob was weary, and thinking that the dog was attracted by some wild creature, paid no attention to him and proceeded to drive Brown Velvet toward the châlet. When he had almost reached the side of the glacier he saw Mr. Walker coming toward him.

"You are going to leave us?" he asked.

"For a time; but I will come again and take charge of Judge Houghton. Don't let him make any excursions in my absence."

"No fear of that; he has had enough,—and I, too." He turned and whistled to his dog, to hide his emotion. "What ails the beast? I believe he is bewitched. If I had not this cow to attend to I would go over and bring him back in my arms, lame as I am from our tramp."

"Wait a few minutes, and I will get him."

Yakob did not say "I thank you," but he looked it; and Mr. Walker sprang cheerily over the ice, never feeling the ache of strained muscles for the great joy which filled his heart. He called the dog, as he approached, but the animal only danced about and whined. He tried to catch him, but he would not be caught, snapping at him viciously when his hand was almost on him. At last he began to wonder what made the animal act so strangely. "Perhaps there is something in the crevasse," and peering over the edge he, too, discovered — Nikolas! Then what a cheer he sent ringing through the air! Yakob understood it. There could be but one meaning to such a triumphant shout; and Yakob gazed at him for a moment, his face transfigured with joy, then forgetting his stiff joints and weariness, and crying, "My boy, my boy!" came leaping across the glacier.

A PEASANT WOMAN OF THE ZERMATT VALLEY.

Mr. Walker looked again at Nikolas, and his heart misgave him. "Is he dead?" he thought; "are we too late?" He walked up and down the edge of the glacier, looking for a way of descent, but soon saw that there was none. He called to Nikolas, but the boy did not rouse; and there was his father coming toward them so joyfully. He could have bitten his tongue for shouting, and yet unaided he could not reach the boy.

Yakob reached him and looked over the brink, his expression of eager hope changing at once to terrified anxiety. "I have my rope with me," he said. "You must lower me into the crevasse."

"You are too heavy," Mr. Walker replied. "I could never hold you."

"True. Then I will lower you — quick!"

Yakob attached the rope, and bracing himself carefully, let Mr. Walker down into the ravine. The young man took up Nikolas, and fastened the rope about him, and Yakob drew his son out of the crevasse. He was so absorbed in bringing the boy to consciousness that he quite forgot that Mr. Walker was still below, and was setting out for home, when he was recalled by a rather impatient shout from the crevasse. He returned quickly, and a moment later Mr. Walker was on the surface. "He is alive!" Yakob exclaimed; "but I must get him to the châlet as quickly as possible. We were not a moment too soon."

Yakob carried his son across the glacier, but at this point his strength gave out, and Mr. Walker bore him up the mountain side to the châlet. It was a strange but joyful little procession which Margaret saw coming as she stepped out into the moonlight for a last view of the valley before retiring. First the good dog, barking loudly, as though he wished to inform the family of the good tidings, then Mr. Walker with Nikolas in his arms, after him Yakob limping along with the assistance of his alpenstock, and last of all the fairy cow, quite tired of her escapade, and following willingly to her manger.

"I have brought him," Mr. Walker exclaimed, as he laid Nikolas in Margaret's arms, "and now I claim your permission to speak — I must not be put off any longer."

"No longer, dear friend," Margaret replied. "It is a night of joy for all of us."

But Mr. Walker did not rest even now. He saw that the exposure to which Nikolas had been subjected had rendered his condition critical, and though nearly worn out by his exertions, he returned to Zermatt for a physician. Fortunately an eminent English surgeon was stopping at one of the hotels, and ordering Walker to bed, he grasped his case of instruments and set out at once for the châlet.

With the exception of badly frozen ears, Nikolas's injuries were found to be slight. When the surgeon had skilfully amputated these enormous deformities, Margaret was surprised to find how the face gained. His long locks would cover the cropping, and the other features had always been good, but he had been in the habit of distorting them with hideous grimaces. Lately, however, a more intellectual expression had come into his face, and as the boy lay sleeping peacefully, Margaret foresaw that it would develop into something very like beauty. He would always be *petite*, but his only deformity now was the twisted ankle, and this the surgeon was sure could be straightened.

Mother Lochwalder and Yakob were full of happiness and gratitude, and were willing to entrust Katchen and Nikolas entirely to Margaret. She accordingly decided that as soon as the Judge and Nikolas were able to travel she would proceed with them and with Katchen to Vevey. Mr. Walker persuaded them to go by way of Mont Blanc, and to reach this point by a little tour into Italy. The recovery was so rapid that in ten days' time they were ready to set out, and the Judge, Margaret, and Mr. Walker took their last view from the favorite lookout.

Just before leaving Margaret remembered Annette's letter. "I must have left it on my lookout just as we discovered Brown Velvet on the glacier."

She went in search with Katchen, but could find no trace of it.

until Katchen cried, "Brown Velvet is munching something over there in the pasture."

The child ran to her and pulled a piece of paper from between her teeth. It was torn and faded; they could just make out that it was Annette's letter, but that was all. Her confession was quite illegible, and Margaret left the Alm, bidding a regretful farewell to Mother Lochwalder, her dear aunt, as she still thought her. Yakob, who had already suggested this trip, went with them as guide as far as Aosta.

CHAPTER XIII.

THE GREAT ST. BERNARD AND MONT BLANC.

> Long could I have stood
> With a religious awe, contemplating
> That house, the highest in the ancient world,
> And destined to perform from age to age
> The noblest service, welcoming as guests
> All of all nations and of every faith —
> A temple sacred to humanity!

> Mont Blanc is the monarch of mountains,
>   They crowned him long ago,
> On a throne of rock in a robe of clouds,
>   With a diadem of snow.

THE party made the excursion on mule-back by way of the Pass of St. Theodule to the village of Breuil, and thence up the Val de Tournache to Chatillon, where they spent the night. All the way they had magnificent views of the Matterhorn and the Italian ranges. The Judge bore the journey in its easy stages very well, and to Nikolas the widening of his horizon seemed and was the opening of a new life.

At Aosta Yakob bade them farewell with tears in his honest eyes, and returned with the mules to Zermatt.

The valley of Aosta is justly celebrated for its beautiful scenery, Mont Blanc rising grandly in the north. Cheever says of it, "I have seen Mont Blanc from all the best points of view, with every advantage; but all taken together, no other view is to be compared for its magnificence with this in the Val d'Aoste."

Margaret came to the conclusion that there were so many sublime and beautiful views among the Alps that comparison was impossible. She could not tell whether the Jungfrau and her wonderful brothers, Monte Rosa, the Matterhorn, or Mont Blanc were the more admirable. She would not rank them, as her grandfather did, according to their height, —

Mont Blanc	15,784 feet.
Monte Rosa	15,223 feet.
The Dom	14,935 feet.
Lyskam	14,889 feet.
Weisshorn	14,804 feet.
Matterhorn	14,705 feet.
Finsetraarhorn	14,039 feet.
Aletschhorn	13,803 feet.
Breithorn	13,685 feet.
Jungfrau	13,671 feet.

It was nothing to her that the Jungfrau stood last in this list of high peaks, and that the Rigi was only 5,905 feet in height, a mere mole-hill in the catalogue. She remembered the mountains by the sensations which they had awakened; and according to this scale the Jungfrau stood first for beauty, and the Matterhorn for terror. Mont Blanc lifted itself now, a monument of solemn thanksgiving and consecration. She could not forget that she had just received her own back from the dead, and that she rode along this beautiful valley in the first days of her betrothal, her life crowned by one of the richest gifts this world can give — a good man's love. Livingston Walker shared the same sentiment of awe. His happiness seemed too great to be true; and often, as his gaze rested on Margaret, there were happy tears in his eyes. The Judge had given his blessing; and although the engagement was referred for its final seal to Margaret's parents, there was no question as to what their answer would be. It would be a long engagement, for he had his way to make in the world. And Margaret knew that the adoption of the two Lochwalder children would make such heavy draughts on her own liberal allowance that her wedding day must be postponed in consequence. But she did not hesitate, nor did her betrothed disapprove the generous action. "It is not generosity at all," Margaret had insisted, "but simple justice, for they are my own family."

And so to both these young people Mont Blanc was the "monarch of mountains," not because it was the highest in Europe, or because the views in its vicinity greatly excelled those of the Jungfrau, the Matterhorn, or the Aletschhorn, from the great glacier where Walker had recently been wandering, but because he had no joy in his heart to keep it warm in that great sepulchral chamber, and because Margaret viewed this scene with infinitely greater elevation of feeling than she had hitherto experienced.

They rested for a day at Aosta, and examined its Roman ruins,— an amphitheatre and a triumphal arch,—for it is a very ancient city, rebuilt by the Emperor Augustus, who stationed here three thousand soldiers, and its name is a corruption of Augusta.

St. Bernard was archdeacon of the cathedral of this city, but left the charming valley, in the year 962, to found the hospice in the cruel mountain pass, for the succor of travellers who, without this shelter, would not infrequently perish in the storms.

This was their next objective point; and here they were hospitably entertained by the monks. Few realize what it is to live always among the snows; for even in summer, water always freezes here in the morning; and in the winter the roads are covered with enormous drifts, sometimes forty feet in depth. Ten or twelve of the brethren of St. Augustine remain here, isolated from the rest of the world, through the dreary winter season. They are all young men, selected for their physical powers; but pneumonia and consumption frequently fasten upon them, and they do not live out the period of their vow, which is fifteen years. Their labors are arduous, and necessitate their going out in all weather. There is a shelter lower down upon the road, where belated travellers frequently take refuge, and the monks visit it with their dogs every morning, and bring any one whom they may find to the convent. A grave young man of eighteen, who had recently taken the vow, showed our travellers the buildings, and explained everything. The hospice is of gray stone, very solid, but bare, and suggesting a penitentiary. The young monk showed them into the parlor, where there was a piano given by the Prince of Wales, and a harmonium, by the composer Blumenthal. This was the first good piano that Nikolas had seen; and he pounced upon it like a bird of prey upon a lamb, and could with difficulty be dragged from it.

"I am glad," said Margaret to the monk, "that you have such a good collection of books with which to while away the weary hours."

The young man smiled. "The hours are indeed weary," he replied; "but not from lack of employment. Besides the work of the house, and the care of our dogs, cows, and mules, the search for the lost, and the entertainment of guests — a never-failing occupation during summer — is the cutting of wood. The difficulty of transportation renders fuel expensive; and we lay in vast stores of fagots, of wood, and of hay, for the winter consumption."

The mention of dogs reminded them of one of the chief attractions of the convent; and they were taken to the kennels, and shown the noble animals who assist the monks in their searches. In 1830 the dogs all perished in a terrific storm, and the breed would have become extinct but for the fact that a pack had been sent to Hollingen, near Berne, which was now returned to the hospice. The monk told them many interesting anecdotes of the sagacity of these dogs, — some of them are occasionally sent out alone, with a little flask of cordial attached to their collars. He said that they showed great uneasiness when the weather was stormy, as though anxious to be sent. When they find an unfortunate they bark loudly, and if not heard, will clear

THE GREAT ST. BERNARD.

the snow from him, and then run back, and by their capering and intelligent actions make themselves understood. The most famous of the St. Bernard dogs was Barry, who rescued forty persons. On one occasion he discovered a little boy, whose mother had been killed by an avalanche, and inducing the little fellow to mount on his back, carried him triumphantly to the convent. The monk told them that this dog, after dying of old age, had been stuffed, and was to be seen at the museum of Berne.

The Judge strongly desired to bring away a pup with him to America, but after considering the matter, decided that the animal would probably be more useful at the hospice than at a New York mansion. "Nikolas and Katchen are pets enough," he said to Margaret. "I must help you in the maintenance of those children, and I will give up the idea of a St. Bernard dog."

How many guests can you entertain?" he asked of the monk, his lecture note-book in hand.

"The hospice has eighty beds," the monk replied, "but we have sheltered as many as five hundred persons in one day, and entertain annually from eight to nine thousand. The heaviest work of the convent was done at the time that Napoleon crossed the Alps in his forced march in May, 1800."

"I have heard that the convent is very rich in estates scattered through Switzerland."

"It was so formerly. In 1480 it was at the height of its prosperity, for it owned ninety-eight livings. Now it possesses only a vineyard at Clarens and a farm at Roch."

The monk next asked them if they would like to visit the morgue, where the bodies of such travellers as are found frozen to death are kept subject to the identification of their friends.

Margaret declined this invitation and remained in the parlor with the children, but the Judge and Mr. Walker visited the melancholy building. Here were many bodies preserved by the cold, dry air; a mother still clasping her babe to her bosom, a strong man with a terrible expression of suffering frozen upon his features, and many others, some crumbling to bone and dust, and others more or less perfect after the lapse of many years.

After a comfortable night's rest our friends passed on their way, the Judge leaving a handsome gratuity in recognition of the hospitality received, and the noble work done for humanity by the monks of St. Bernard.

"If anybody had told me," he said, as they rode away, "that I, a member of the Presbyterian Church, in good and regular standing, would contribute to the support of a popish monastery, I would have thought that either he or I had gone insane."

As they emerged from the pass into the Rhone Valley, they were reminded of Dr. Bartol's remarks on the Pass of St. Bernard:—

"In this as in the other passes, one is struck with the thought that God never builds up in the world an insuperable wall, but provides everywhere for his creatures an exit, some way of escape. Wide and deep from the valley of the Rhone opens the solemn door of the pass as for an army to march along.

"The Pass of the Splügen stands alone in the ghastly grandeur of the Via Mala, or Evil Way, where, betwixt opposing precipices, in some places nearly a third of a mile in height and often only a few yards apart, extending through a space of more than four miles, the most wonderful engineering has built a road along gulfs which it might be thought possible to span with nothing larger than a thread in the mouth of a carrier dove. Surely we can at length pass anywhere, out of whatsoever difficulty, if we have been able to pass here."

"There is one range of mountains before me," said Walker, "through which I do not as yet see any pass. I mean my future. I have prepared myself thoroughly as a civil and mining engineer. I hope to find employment in the western part of the United States,

BARRY, THE BRAVE DOG OF ST. BERNARD.

but as yet the way seems shut by an impenetrable wall. However, I shall not be discouraged, but look for the pass. You have mentioned the Pass of the Splügen. I went over it this summer by diligence, and the awful beauty of the Via Mala fully justifies what has been written of it."

"Tell me more of that trip," Margaret asked. "So much of consequence has happened that I have not heard as much as I would like of your summer wanderings."

"From the Splügen I pursued a northeast course through the beautiful valley of the Engadine to Innsbruck, thence to Salzburg, from which city I made a flying pilgrimage to the lakes of the Tyrol, — the Königsee, the Obersee, and the Traunsee. At the Salz-Kammergat, one of the most interesting salt-mines in the world, I met a young Austrian who interested me in some lead-mines in Hungary. I had remarked on the terrible condition of the miners, and he told me that what interested him at these other mines was not the engineering, which seemed to him rather old-fashioned, but the attempt made by the owner to alleviate the condition of his laborers. As my chance acquaintance, a Herr Hauptman in the Austrian army, was on his way back to his post, I determined to accompany him, and see something of the enterprise in question."

Margaret had been listening with increasing interest.

"What was the name of the mines and of their owner?" she asked.

"The mines were called Nagy Krajova. I believe Nagy means 'great,' and Krajova is the family name of the nobleman who is the owner of the estate, the Count Krajova Lajos, putting the Christian name last according to the Hungarian fashion."

"Delightful!" Margaret exclaimed. "I knew as soon as you began to tell about them that it must be Lajos. Did you really visit the mines? And had he begun reforms? He told me that he intended to institute them, but he did not talk as if he had already accomplished anything."

"Indeed he has accomplished a great deal. I know of no miners whose families live in as comfortable cottages and have as much done for their well-being. While I was there an order came to erect a new building, which is to serve as schoolhouse and public library. I was sorry not to see the gentleman, but they told me he was travelling in Switzerland."

"You had a glimpse of him at Glion, the evening you passed us by with such disdain," Margaret replied, mischievously. "He is a delightful man, and we learned to know him well and like him immensely, *almost* as well as a certain scornful scholar of my acquaintance."

"However admirable he may be as a philanthropist," Mr. Walker replied, with a trace of pique, "he is the most unpractical man for the proprietor of a large mine of any that I know. It only proves what I have often heard, that a man cannot attend to everybody's business and his own at the same time."

"I like the Count Lajos all the better," Margaret replied, with some warmth, "for first thinking of the welfare of those dependent upon him."

"It seems to me that the first concern of a business man is his business, and there are immense resources in the count's mine if they were only properly developed. I do not mean to the prejudice of his workmen, but simply by the application of modern methods."

"Then it seems to me that Count Lajos and you ought to be rolled into one man. Seriously, Livingston, I fancy that I have some influence with him and that he might engage you as overseer of his mine, perhaps even take you into partnership if I asked it."

"Please do not think of it. I do not wish to owe my advancement in life to wire-pulling, and still less would I be willing that you should put yourself in the position of asking so great a favor from this man."

He did not say aloud, "whose successful rival I am," but he thought it, and with no feeling of vexation with Margaret. "Who could help loving her?" he thought. "Poor Count Krajova, I am richer than you."

Their next stopping-place was the Valley of Chamouni, which they reached by a delightful drive by way of the Tête Noir.

A well-known author has said that it is useless to use mountainous words to present mountainous things, and the beauties of this celebrated valley have been too often described, both in prose and verse, to need an extended account here. The monarch of mountains rose grandly before them, but Margaret was disappointed to find in the valley a collection of fashionable hotels like those of Interlaken, with all the modern conveniences and inconveniences of porters, telephones, electric bells, and waiters in evening dress.

THE BARON.

"It has been well said," Mr. Walker remarked, "that a gentleman is only to be distinguished from his valet by his aristocratic expression of innocuous imbecility."

BARONESS OF HOHENSCHLOSSE.

"Switzerland is indeed the summer-house of the world," Margaret replied, "and this is just the place for 'Calumet and Hecla' to appear again." That very afternoon they caught a glimpse of the familiar face, which bore now the unfamiliar name of the Baroness of Hohenschlosse.

The listless expression changed to a momentary gleam of pleasure as she recognized Margaret. She dropped her husband's arm presently and came to the part of the veranda where Margaret was sitting.

"I am married," she said, with a little flash of pride. "I am really a baroness now. Mother has gone back to America. *He* did not want her to live with us. I'm so sorry you didn't marry that handsome count; then I could have seen you now and then. I foresee that I shall be a little lonely, for *he* wants me to drop my American friends; but if you were a countess he would let you visit me. Good by; he is beckoning to me."

"And to think," Margaret said to herself with deep self-scorn, "that when I was in Lucerne I was like *that!*"

The Judge manifested no desire to climb Mont Blanc, though Mr. Walker assured him that it was not so dangerous as the Matterhorn. "It has been made this season," he informed the Judge, "by several Americans; and among others by Dr. John S. White of New York, and by his son, a Harvard student, whose intellectual and athletic prowess at the age of seventeen are alike remarkable. It has also been made by ladies. The first was a French woman, Mademoiselle d'Angeville, who accomplished it in 1840. The rarity of the atmosphere frequently causes a giddiness, and even temporary insanity, which is known to the guides as the mountain sickness. It is an expensive trip, for besides provisions and equipments, four or more guides must be engaged, at twenty dollars apiece."

"TO THINK THAT I WAS LIKE THAT!"

"None of my money shall go in that way," said the cautious Judge. "Experience is the best school-teacher; but she's a very expensive one, as I have ascertained."

The remainder of the party improved the day — a remarkably clear one — by climbing to a sightly point called "The Chapeau," a cliff opposite Montanvert, where a hut had been erected for the use of travellers; and here one clear day they enjoyed a picnic and a magnificent view of the mighty Mer de Glace, formed by the union of three glaciers, and not inappropriately named; for its sharp pinnacles are not unlike the stormy waves of an angry sea.

"I think Shelley has best described this spot," said Margaret, reading the following selection made for the Judge's note-book: —

> "The glaciers creep
> Like snakes that watch their prey from their far fountains,
> Slowly rolling on; there many a precipice,
> Frost and the sun in scorn of mortal power
> Have piled dome, pyramid, and pinnacle;
> A city of death, distinct with many a tower
> And wall impregnable of beaming ice.
> Yet not a city; but a flood of ruin
> Is there, that from the boundaries of the sky
> Rolls its perpetual stream; vast pines are strewing
> Its destined path, or in the mangled soil
> Branchless and shattered stand; the rocks, drawn down
> From yon remotest waste, have overthrown
> The limits of the dead and living world,
> Never to be reclaimed."

"The Glacier des Bossons at Chamouni is a striking example of the exactitude with which the progressive motion has been calculated by scientists," said Mr. Walker. "Dr. Hamel and three guides were swept away by an avalanche, and buried deeply upon this glacier in the summer of 1822. It was impossible to recover their bodies; but Professor Forbes, on examining the locality where they perished, foretold that, according to his rate of glacier motion, they would appear at the bottom of the glacier in forty years. In 1862 relatives and friends of the lost men, as well as scientists anxious to investigate the truth of this theory, were on the spot, and many relics of the party were discovered: a lantern, a straw hat, a luncheon done up carefully, parts of a ladder, and several bodies, one of which was recognized."

"I think," said Margaret, "that the incident has been utilized in a novel. A young man is lost in this way, and after the lapse of forty years, his betrothed revisits the spot, and is confronted by his fresh young face, preserved unchanged in the snow, while her own has grown wrinkled and old."

"I read in the Boston *Transcript* of a terrible accident which occurred here in 1870," continued Mr. Walker. "Three travellers, two of whom were Americans, John C. Randall of Quincy, Mass., and Dr. James B. Beane, a young physician of Baltimore, with three guides and four porters, attempted the ascent, and were all lost. The trip requires two days, and the party had spent the first night at the shelter of Les Grands Mulets, setting the usual signal to inform watchers below of their safe arrival. They completed the ascent the next morning, and were seen in the afternoon descending the mountain. Suddenly, as those who watched described it, a veil seemed to be thrown over them, and they disappeared.

"At night no lights were shown at the Grand Mulets, and the worst fears were indulged. At five o'clock the next morning a relief party of thirty was organized and started out. They encountered a terrific tempest of sleet and snow, and were out all the following night, throwing the village of Chamouni into a panic of apprehension for their safety. They returned, however, after a fruitless search, reporting that such quantities of snow had fallen that all land-marks were covered, and that no human being could have survived such a night on the upper part of the mountain. Several days later the bodies of some of the party were found. They were seated, and Dr. Beane held a note-book containing several entries. The last, dated the night of the storm, was this: 'We have dug a grotto in the snow at a height of 15,000 feet. I have no hope of descending; my feet are frozen and I am exhausted. I have only strength to write these words. I die believing in Jesus Christ, with the sweet thought of my family, my friendships, and all. I hope we shall meet in heaven.'"

A little silence fell on the party after reading these words. The escape of the Judge and Nikolas was so recent that they seemed to bear a personal import.

"What did you think of, Nikolas," Margaret asked, "as you lay in the ravine just before you were rescued?"

"I did not think that I was going to die," the boy replied. "I remembered the story you told me of the angels appearing to the shepherds, and the last thing that I remember is wondering if they would come and lift me out, and thinking that perhaps we had made a mistake in keeping cows instead of sheep, because the angels loved shepherds better than cow-keepers. That was foolish, was it not? Now I know that the good angels love us all."

CHAPTER XIV.

THE FÊTE DES VIGNERONS.

> With antics and with fooleries,
>   With clappings and with laughter,
> They fill the streets of Burgos;
>   And the devil he comes after.
> For the King had hired the hornèd fiend,
>   For fifteen maravedis;
> And there he goes, with hoofs for toes,
>   To terrify the ladies.
> LOCKHART'S "Spanish Ballads."

ANNETTE, driven by an accusing conscience, had gone to Baireuth to make her confession to Cecilia. She had written a full statement of her deception, and left it for Margaret to read; but she could not bear to face Margaret with it. Cecilia, we know, had always exercised a good influence over Annette, and to her she went in her hour of remorse. She hoped, too, to find the mysterious countess, and through her to ascertain all the facts in regard to Margaret's aunt, and thus make some reparation for her fault.

Brown Velvet, it will be remembered, had eaten up Annette's written confession, and Margaret was now approaching Vevey, having completed the circle of her Swiss tour in entire ignorance of her real position. The countess and her party had left Baireuth before Annette's arrival, but Cecilia received her kindly, heard the miserable story patiently, and while she did not attempt to lessen the girl's realization of her sin, helped her earnestly in her repentant efforts. Letters were immediately dispatched to the countess and to Lajos.

Cecilia remembered that the name of Margaret Du Fais, which Annette now declared was that of Margaret's great-aunt, was that of the countess's old friend, of whose property Lajos was the guardian.

"Have you any proof of this?" Cecilia had asked, "other than your own statement?"

"I have the letter of Margaret's aunt," Annette replied. "I took it from the desk just before leaving New York, for I had an idea that it might be useful in some way."

"It will be very useful in identifying the Baroness Du Fais," Cecilia replied. And she accordingly added a postcript to her letter to the countess, asking her if she possessed any scrap of her friend's writing to send it, that the chirography might be compared.

"This information is sure to create grave complications," she said to Annette; "and you must wait here until we hear from the countess."

An answer came in a few days in the person of Lajos himself. He had hardly more than arrived at home, when the news came, but it was of such importance, that he dropped his plans for improving the condition of the miners, and returned immediately to Baireuth. He reported the countess as completely prostrated by the shock. She was unable to travel, but sent in her stead the family lawyer, Kisfaludy Janos. Annette's deposition was taken, and the letter in her possession compared with several sent by the countess, and found to be in the same delicate but eccentric script. The statements in the baroness's letter tallied exactly with the facts which were known to exist, and a crowning proof was the seal, the mailed hand bearing the firebrand, which Lajos recognized at once as the crest of his aunt's friend.

The next step was to apprise Margaret. Annette persisted that she had already done so, but a letter arrived from Margaret at this juncture, written from the hospice of St. Bernard, reminding Cecilia that the time was approaching when they had agreed to meet at Vevey, and speaking of Katchen and Nikolas as her cousins. Cecilia read this letter to Annette, and the girl was overwhelmed, at first with joy at the news that Nikolas was saved, and then with fear lest Margaret should decide to have nothing to do with the children when she ascertained that they were not her relatives.

"She was so fond of Nikolas," Annette said, "that long after I regretted my deception, I kept it up for his sake, for she had planned to do such great things for him. I do not think I would ever have had the courage to confess if I had not thought that he was dead, and my confession could do him no harm."

Annette determined that she would go to Vevey with Cecilia to take the children back to Zermatt in case Margaret wished to give them up. Now that she had eased her conscience by confession, she felt that she could even endure seeing Margaret, and the Hungarian lawyer was of the opinion that as chief witness in the affair, her presence was necessary until it was entirely settled.

A STUDENT OF BERNE.

The four accordingly set out together. As they were a little in advance of the appointed time of meeting, Cecilia and Annette stopped for two days in Berne, the capital of the Swiss Confederacy, the impatient Lajos hurrying on with his lawyer to Vevey.

Had we time and space, an interesting chapter might be given to this ancient city, and to an explanation of the Swis government, which in many respects resembles that of the United States of America.

A republican constitution was formed in 1848, against which the monarchies of Europe protested without effect. Twenty-two little cantons form the Swiss Republic; some of them are not larger than American counties, and the entire number of inhabitants scarcely exceeds three millions. It is a republic in miniature, but its citizens have a more direct power in making their own laws than those of our own country.

HIGH STREET, BERNE.

Should thirty thousand citizens or eight cantons disapprove of any law made by the Parliament it must be submitted to popular vote.

"The people, not the president, hold the final veto power in Switzerland." Indeed he has very little power of any kind and is only elected for one year. It is said that a session of the Swiss Parliament is a curious spectacle; for the discussions are conducted in all three of the languages used in the confederation,— French, German, and Italian. The official interpreters repeat every remark made, translating it into the other languages so that all the members may understand.[1]

The new parliament houses are very handsome, but Cecilia was more interested in the antique architecture of the city.

She stood before the clock tower at noon and watched the procession of puppets, the knight in armor, and the bears, which file out as chimes strike the hour of twelve; and she drank of the ogre fountain, erected to commemorate the possibly mythical story of the murder of a child by the Jews.

Cecilia and Annette reached Glion only to find that every room in the house was taken, and that she had carelessly neglected to secure her own. A glance at the register reassured her; Margaret was here, and she asked to be shown to her room.

Margaret was delighted to share her room with her friend, and ordered a mattress laid upon the floor of her little dressing-room for Annette, which was the best that could be done in the way of hospitality. They slept little that night, however, for each of the girls had a great deal to say. Lajos had not yet found Margaret, so that Cecilia had the pleasure of first communicating the news.

"I do not quite understand what it all means," Margaret said, after the first shock was over; "but one thing is certain, I shall not give up the children. As for Annette, I forgive her freely. Like Joseph's brethren, she 'thought evil, but God meant it for good.' I never could have understood in any other way how the poor live, or have sympathized with their troubles so intimately if I had not believed

---

[1] The author is indebted for information in regard to the Swiss government to an article by S. H. M. Byers, published in the *Youth's Companion* for March, 1889.

that I shared them. And after all, are we not of one great family?"

Annette, who was at her old trick of listening at the door, could not contain her gratitude, but burst in and threw herself at Margaret's feet, weeping and blessing her.

Margaret was deeply affected. "There, Cousin Annette, that will do," she said. "We will not tell Mother Lochwalder or Yakob anything about this. I will be their 'lady cousin' still. Go back and care for them while they live, and rest assured that Katchen and Nikolas are as dear to me as ever."

KATCHEN AMERICANIZED.

Although Lajos and Mr. Kisfaludy had arrived at Glion for two days before this, it so happened that they had not yet met Margaret; for, owing to the crowded state of the hotel, they had been obliged to take a room at a hotel at Montreux. Lajos had twice mounted the hill to call upon Margaret, but had not found her at home. He had written her, asking her to appoint an hour when he might call; but the clerk had so much to attend to that he forgot to deliver the letter, and it was not until the latter part of the *fête* that good fortune brought them together.

The festival lasted five days, beginning on the 12th of August, with spectacles on the mornings of four of the days. On Wednesday, the 14th, there was a performance in the evening; but the day was reserved as a rest for the performers. The Judge had secured tickets, some time in advance, at five dollars each, for seats in the great amphitheatre for Thursday.

Every means of conveyance from Glion was packed; but here, too, our friends had been so wise as to secure a carriage on their first arrival. They left Glion early in the morning, passed many pedestrians on their way, and many vehicles filled beyond their capacity. The boats were loaded to the water's edge; and though extra trains were run, hundreds of disappointed passengers were left standing upon the platforms of the stations. At the entrance to the out-of-door theatre it was still worse. Although the seats, erected upon scaffolding three stories high, contained twelve thousand persons, four or five thousand who arrived on Wednesday were unable to obtain admission.

AT THE FESTIVAL.

Three sides of the vast enclosure were framed by the tiers of seats. The fourth side was occupied by three monumental entrances dedicated to Pallas, Bacchus, and Ceres. The background was formed by the beautiful line of the mountains. At exactly a quarter of eight an hundred handsome Switzers in national costume, preceded by a band of music, marched in, and took positions on each side. They were received with the enthusiastic applause of their compatriots, some of whom were heard to express the wish that Bismarck might have seen them. "Yes," said one sturdy Bernese, "he would see then what stuff our boys are made of, and would not talk so lightly of suppressing the Swiss Republic by force of arms." While the bells of the town rang eight o'clock the three *cortèges* of Spring, Summer, and Autumn made their entrance amidst the salvos of artillery.

After a Swiss hymn chanted by the full chorus, and the invocations of the high priests, dances were executed by each of the three companies, commencing by the "Children of Spring," charming little cherubs from five to eight years of age. Then the mowers, robed in sky-blue, simulated the cutting of grass, and shepherds and shepherdesses, costumed in pale rose, led in beautiful troops of snow-white lambs. The gardeners next appeared, bearing arches twined with roses, forming a lovely arbor through which troops of pretty girls danced merrily. Then, filling the air with the bray of their mighty Alpine horns, came the herdsmen and dairy-maids, conducting beautiful cows, and here Nikolas's enthusiasm knew no bounds, though he declared that none of the prize animals was so handsome as Brown Velvet. A celebrated singer of Fribourg sang the Ranz des Vaches. The suite which accompanied Spring ended, and a group of haymakers dressed in red, carrying scythes and forks, gleaners in white bearing sheaves, and thrashers with flails, did honor to

TAKING IT ALL IN.

the goddess Summer, while a great mill came tottering in to complete the representation. To represent Autumn, a pretty ballet was danced to music by vintagers who executed all the processes of gathering grapes and placing them in baskets which the boys emptied into a wine-press. Then came the triumphal car of Bacchus, escorted by a company of dancing Bacchantes, fauns and thyrsus-bearers.

To close the performance and to stand for Winter, a village marriage procession was enacted. Among the guests were the twenty-two Swiss cantons dressed in the peasant costume appropriate to each.

The notary, in a black satin gown, followed; then a group of fiddlers and pretty children bearing the wedding presents; a dowry-wagon, loaded with the bride's furniture, and a band of huntsmen. It was a beautiful spectacle, and one which fully justified the enthusiastic praises which the countess had bestowed upon a former representation. Margaret was very glad that their tour in Switzerland had chanced to include this privilege.

But after the close of the performance the utmost confusion reigned. Passengers for Lausanne were obliged to wait for several hours at the railway station, though long trains of forty-five cars and three locomotives had been provided. At the landings it was still worse. On the frail wharf without a railing were crowded hundreds of people desiring to embark in different directions, so that when the steamer for Geneva arrived many were borne on board by the press, and carried away who had an entirely opposite destination.

In attempting to reach their carriage Margaret was separated from her friends, and was not able to find them for an hour. Judging that they would come in search of her, she stationed herself in a doorway near the entrance to the grounds of the festival, and waited.

The crowd had partially dispersed when two gentlemen passed her. One of them glanced back over his shoulder when at a little distance, uttered an exclamation and hurriedly returned. It was Lajos, who had sought for her for four days without success. He introduced his companion, the lawyer Kisfaludy. Mutual explanations were made, and Lajos secured for them all a more convenient coigne of vantage in the window of a cobbler's shop. Here, where they could still keep a lookout for her friends, Lajos left the lawyer in care of Margaret, while he hurried away in search of the Judge.

"Before I go," he said, "let me give my aunt's message. She begs that you will accept her apologies for—"

"None are necessary, Friend Lajos."

"It is like you to say so. We think differently. I owe you a

VINTAGE FESTIVAL, VEVEY.

large debt outside the moneyed one. We will talk it all over at any time which will be convenient to you." And with a respectful bow, he was gone.

The lawyer, a quizzical-appearing little man, regarded Margaret with keen inquiry. She could not help thinking that he looked exactly like a barrister in a play. He spoke excellent English, and began at once to discuss the new situation.

"It is very fortunate for you, mademoiselle, that the discovery of the existing relations between yourself and the Baroness Du Fais was made so exactly in the nick of time."

"How is that?" Margaret asked.

KISFALUDY JANOS.

"The will of your respected great-aunt," explained the little man, "provided — and that of the late Count Krajova made a similar provision — that if you preferred your claim as heiress to the baroness's estate at any time before the fifth of August of this year, one of three results should ensue. Case first: should a marriage be arranged between you and the Count Lajos, the estates of the late count and baroness would pass to you both jointly."

"That case is impossible," Margaret replied promptly.

"Exactly so. Now observe what follows. The estates pass *in toto* from whichever party declines the marriage to the party consenting thereto."

"Then," said Margaret, "I do not see that I am the gainer by this will; for I certainly decline this marriage."

"My dear young lady, I will imagine that I have not heard that remark; for it is so greatly detrimental to your own interests that it should not be made without due deliberation."

"But nothing could induce me to marry the Count Lajos, much as I esteem him as a friend."

"Very good. There will be no necessity for you to do so. The Count Lajos has already declined to marry you. Your acknowledging yourself ready to carry out the provisions of this clause will not prejudice your future otherwise than to secure to yourself a valuable estate."

"This is very astonishing," Margaret replied. "I must consult with Livingston — with my grandfather, I mean — I must think it over."

"Exactly so. And, as I see the count approaching with a gentleman, we will drop the subject."

"I have found your party," said Lajos; "and, at the same time, a gentleman whom I have been in search of for some time. I have heard a great deal of Mr. Livingston Walker, both from Miss Newton, and, latterly, from a friend of mine, who tells me that he showed him our mines during my absence. I hope to have further conversation with you, sir, on the subject of mining engineering."

An appointment was made for a meeting on the following day, at Glion; and Margaret, quite dazed by what had happened, was escorted by Mr. Walker to her carriage.

She said nothing to her betrothed, or to the Judge, in regard to Mr. Kisfaludy's communication. It seemed to her, in spite of what she had said, that this was a matter which she must decide for herself, and that it could be decided honorably in only one way. She dreaded her grandfather's legal sophistries; for she knew that he would regret her loss of the fortune, and would strive in every way to place it in her possession.

Lajos and the lawyer arrived at the appointed time, and, leaving the latter to explain the will to the Judge and to Mr. Walker, Margaret asked Lajos to take a short walk with her in the grounds of the hotel.

"Kisfaludy Janos tells me that he has informed you of the peculiar position in which we stand to each other," said Lajos.

"Yes," replied Margaret, "and I have no doubt that it seems as absurd to you as it does to me."

"It does seem as if our loving relatives, while they had our best interests at heart, muddled matters about as effectually as possible."

"But the solution is very simple. I refuse you, Lajos. You won't mind it, I am sure, under the circumstances, and you are free and have the fortune besides."

"I beg your pardon, Margaret; it is impossible for you to refuse one who has never proposed for your hand."

Margaret flushed. "But you won't mind doing so when I assure you beforehand that it is simply a matter of form, to secure your estates. I pledge you my word that I will certainly decline your offer."

"I believe you, my friend; but nevertheless I am not free to make one. I am betrothed to Alice. It would be dishonorable for me, as her promised husband, to propose for the hand of any other woman. Therefore, Margaret, the mines are yours. I only ask that you will try to perfect the reforms which I have instituted."

Margaret tapped her foot impatiently. "Don't you see that the conditions are the same for both of us? I cannot own the estate without first stating that I am willing to marry you."

"And why not, since I have no desire to take advantage of that admission. You cannot fear, Margaret, that you are being led into a trap?"

"Oh! no, indeed; I am quite convinced that nothing could induce you to marry me, and it is very lovely of you. But then, you see, I can't even pretend to consent to this marriage, for I am engaged to Mr. Walker."

Each of the young people looked at each other in comical perplexity, and then burst into a merry peal of laughter.

"Here's a pretty state of things," Lajos remarked at last. "I don't believe there ever existed just such another complication. We shall have to leave it to be settled by wiser heads than our own. Let us go in and see what your grandfather and Kisfaludy Janos can make of it."

They found the others awaiting their coming with serious faces.

Mr. Walker in especial seemed ill pleased by the information which he had just received. His face lightened, however, as Margaret announced: "And Lajos and I wish it distinctly understood that under no circumstances whatever can we or could we marry each other, for we each of us love some one else a thousand times more. And the old mines are of no consequence whatever."

"The question at issue then," said the lawyer, "is as to the priority of this decision."

"I decided first," said Lajos promptly. "I decided that I cared more for Alice than for any other good fortune, when I first met her at Glion. The estate clearly belongs to Margaret."

"But I decided at the same time," said Margaret, "that, although you are a very nice friend, Lajos, no fortune would induce me to marry you."

"Children, cease your quarrelling," said the Judge; "we shall never come to a conclusion in this way. Was there not a third clause in the will, Mr. Janos?"

"Kisfaludy," Lajos corrected. "Janos is his Christian name, John, which we Hungarians write last."

"Absurd custom!" growled the Judge. "Well, Mr. Kiss-the-lady,—you have not read us the entire will, I believe."

"The third provision related to the possibility of the heiress not appearing before the fifth of August of this year. It reads as follows:—

"Copies of both of these wills shall be sent to Miss Margaret Du Fais in the United States of America. And if the said Margaret Du Fais shall decease before her coming of age, or shall not present her claim, or it shall not be preferred by her legal representatives before the fifth of August, 1889, then the party of the second part, Krajova Lajos, shall be released from any obligations of betrothal by us entered into, and from the conditions of property settlement stated in clauses first and second, but the original amount left by Margaret Du Fais, Baroness, shall be rendered to her said grandniece, her heirs or assigns, without interest, at any time after the said fifth of August, 1889, on which claim to the same shall be made."

"Strange, that we never received a copy of the wills, but that certainly is the fairest thing all around," said the Judge. "It is now the fifteenth of August, you will observe."

"Unfortunately," replied Kisfaludy, "information was received by us as to the identity of Miss Du Fais with the proofs contained in the confession of Annette Stauffer on the third of August."

"Information, true," exclaimed Margaret, "but no claim was preferred. *I* did not even authorize the sending of the information, and the will expressly states that the claim must be preferred by me or by my legal representatives. Clearly the circumstances fall under the third clause."

"I believe you are right, young lady, and that it will be so decided by our courts," remarked Kisfaludy.

"Then, Margaret," said Lajos, "we shall be equal owners of the mines. In what form would you like to have your property rendered?"

"There will be time enough to settle that," said Kisfaludy, "after the will is duly approved by law; but that is an easy matter now."

And so the conference broke up, and in this way the knotty problem was at last settled.

Lajos urged them all to accept his aunt's invitation to visit at the chateau until everything was settled, but the Judge and Margaret were eager to return to America. It was finally agreed that Mr. Walker should represent Margaret's interests as Lajos's partner and superintendent of the mines, Margaret's funds not to be drawn from the works, as Mr. Walker believed that they were well invested there, and that with more progressive management might be made to yield a handsome income for all concerned.

"I shall be glad of this," said Margaret, "for now I can educate my protégées, and Nikolas can have the best surgical treatment."

"And our marriage need not be postponed to an indefinite future.

I shall return to America next year to render an account of my stewardship, and if my report is satisfactory shall claim my reward."

Thus ended the travels of the Three Vassar Girls in Switzerland.

From Glion Lajos, Mr. Kisfaludy, and Mr. Walker returned to Hungary. The others crossed the lake to Geneva, from which point they had begun their Swiss tours.

While here, and just before returning to America, it chanced that the Judge and Margaret passed the shop where the Judge had purchased his alpenstock, and had so confidently ordered it to be branded with the names of the most celebrated Alpine peaks. "I shall have the shaft sand-papered," said the Judge humbly; "for even before the rival members of the New York Geographical Society I cannot show quite the effrontery which is ascribed to an English mountaineer by Henry Glassford Bell in his poem: —

"MY ALPENSTOCK.

"Best of artists, mark for me
 On my trusty alpenstock
All the proper things, d'ye see?
 Every mountain, every rock.

"That when I go home therewith
 Friends may know that I have been
Quite as high as Albert Smith,
 Or balloon of Mr. Green.

"Mark it with the Rigi first;
 Some say that's an easy hill,
Yet I own the place accurst
 Found me at the bottom still.

"Then the Brunig — mark it strong;
 Truth itself can't take offence.
All that height I came along,
 Rattling in the diligence.

THE FÊTE DES VIGNERONS.

"Mark it with the Jungfrau next—
  Very few have ventured on her.
That I did not I am vext,
  For I meant it, on my honor.

"From Martigny by Tête Noir
  Or the Col de Balme they pace.
I said only *au revoir*,
  When I saw the kind of place.

"Mark it lastly with Mont Blanc,
  Though it made me gasp and quake
With a kind of mortal pang,
  Just to view it from the lake.

"Thanks, my artist! Now I go
  Back to London with delight,
For my alpenstock will show
  What becomes a man of might."

www.ingramcontent.com/pod-product-compliance
Lightning Source LLC
Chambersburg PA
CBHW021012240426
43669CB00037B/630